Epistemology
A Beginner's Guide

ONEWORLD BEGINNER'S GUIDES combine an original, inventive, and engaging approach with expert analysis on subjects ranging from art and history to religion and politics, and everything in-between. Innovative and affordable, books in the series are perfect for anyone curious about the way the world works and the big ideas of our time.

Epistemology
A Beginner's Guide

Robert M. Martin

ONEWORLD

A Oneworld Paperback Original

Published by Oneworld Publications 2010
Reprinted, 2015, 2018, 2020, 2023

Copyright © 2010

ISBN 978–1–85168–732–9
eISBN 978–1–78074–154–3

Typeset by Jayvee, Trivandrum, India
Cover design by vaguelymemorable.com
Printed and bound in Great Britain by Clays Ltd, Elcograf S.p.A.

Oneworld Publications
10 Bloomsbury Street
London WC1B 3SR
England

To Fran

Acknowledgments

My thanks to Mike Harpley and the anonymous reviewer at Oneworld for their helpful criticisms and suggestions.

Contents

Introduction

Everybody knows things. But what exactly is knowledge? What's missing when some beliefs don't count as knowledge? Where does knowledge come from? Why are some sources of belief reliable sources for knowledge? Are *any* sources reliable? It's surprising – given how ordinary and everyday knowledge is – that the answers are not obvious. Philosophers have been thinking about these questions, and arguing with each other about what the answers are, for at least two thousand years. We'll take a look at the main things – the most interesting things – they've had to say.

An unusual thing about philosophy is that there's debate about *everything*, from the very beginning. This makes philosophy very different from other fields, which start with elementary facts and techniques that everyone agrees on, and that students new to the subject are expected to accept and master without question. You should not read this book expecting to find out the universally accepted elementary groundwork – there isn't any in philosophy. What there is, instead, is a series of questions, each with several different answers proposed by various philosophers.

Some readers unfamiliar with this sort of thing would be tempted to look among the various responses to find the one the author really wants the reader to believe in. This response will be frustrated: the author of this book has made a strong effort to disguise his own opinions. You won't be able to guess what he thinks – and there's really no point in trying. (Who cares what *he* thinks?) Or else you might give up on trying to figure out which answers are right and which are wrong. This response will make things boring – if you don't try to judge which answer is right, that takes away much of the interest in what these philosophers say.

The best response to this book is to try to evaluate every position – to judge whether it's correct or not. This is not just a gut reaction: every position presented will be accompanied by arguments pro and con – arguments you can consider, to see whether they're convincing. Maybe you'll be able to add some arguments of your own.

If any of these issues grips you enough, you can go far deeper into this issue than what's here by looking into what philosophers have had to say in other books and philosophy journals. At the end of the book, you'll find a section telling you where to find the writings which are the sources of some positions and quotations, and where to start reading further about the main issues.

In a way, then, this book offers you something not available from introductions to many other fields. Here you can start *doing* philosophy – evaluating different positions, trying to answer questions, thinking critically and creatively – from the very beginning. This can be an exhilarating experience.

The official name for the study of knowledge in philosophy is **epistemology**. The word '**epistemological**' means *pertaining to the study of knowledge*; while '**epistemic**' means *pertaining to knowledge*. These are handy bits of philosophy-jargon, which we'll be using in the rest of this book.

Defining 'knowledge'

Senses of 'know'

The first question we ought to think about is: what, exactly, is knowledge? That is, when is it proper to say that someone *knows* something? What we're after, here, is an account of what it takes to be knowledge. Sometimes it's thought that to give this account we must provide a set of conditions that are individually necessary and jointly sufficient.

A condition is **necessary** for being x when something can't be x unless it satisfies that condition. *Being female* is a necessary condition for being your sister; nobody could be your sister unless that person is female. A single condition is **sufficient** for x when anything that satisfies that condition would be an x. *Being a daughter of your aunt* is sufficient for *being your cousin* (but notice that it's not necessary). Two or more conditions are **jointly sufficient** for x when anything that satisfies all those conditions would be an x. These conditions: *being female* and *having the same parents as you do*, are jointly sufficient for being your sister. Anyone who satisfies both these conditions is your sister.

The noun 'knowledge' and the verb 'to know' are used in a large variety of ways. The *Oxford English Dictionary* devotes almost 2600 words to defining various senses and constructions involving the verb (not including hundreds of examples). It's difficult to sort all this out, but we can roughly distinguish three main kinds of ways of knowing, corresponding to three sorts of things said to be known:

1 **Knowledge of facts** (for example, *Fred knows that the party is cancelled*). We'll call this **knowing-that**.
2 **Knowledge of a thing or person** (for example, *I know Sally; Irving knows every song the Beatles recorded*). We'll call this **knowing-him/her/it**.
3 **Knowledge how to do something** (for example, *Zelda knows how to string a guitar*). We'll call this **knowing-how**.

This may seem very clear and straightforward, but even here, at the very beginning of our subject, what seems obvious may not be correct, and it's not easy to say what really is correct. First, let's look at a sample of some of the meanings 'know' can have; see if you can sort them into those three categories.

You can be said to know when:

you can distinguish between two things
you can perform an action
you're acquainted with something
you're aware of a fact
you're aware of a thing
you're able to identify someone
you're able to reidentify someone you've seen earlier
you're familiar or intimate with someone
you have information about something
you have learned something
you have practical understanding of something
you recognize a statement as true.

Can you sort these into the three categories? It's difficult, maybe impossible. Maybe the three categories aren't inclusive enough.

Next, think about what might be involved in sense 2. When you say that you know Sally, what exactly does that mean? Well, it can mean that you can recognize her when you see her; or that you know that she's intelligent, moody, and creative; or that you know how to cheer her up when she's down; or a number of other things. Knowledge in sense 2, then, can involve *knowing-that* and *knowing-how*. Is it ever (or always) entirely a matter of *knowing-that* plus *knowing-how*?

Now think about 3. What is it to know guitar-stringing? Perhaps this case of *knowing-how* is actually a matter of *knowing-that* (sense 1). Zelda knows that the strings need to be inserted into the pegs with the loose end under the winding, that the thickest string goes on the top end, and so on. Are some cases of *knowing-how* just cases of *knowing that*?

What we have noticed here is that some cases of 2 may really amount just to cases of 1 or 3, and that some cases of 3 may really amount just to cases of 1. This suggests that we don't really need three categories at all: maybe all knowing is just a case of *knowing-that*, category 1.

But on the other hand, there do appear to be cases of 2 and 3 that can't eventually be collapsed into case 1. Consider this example of case 2: 'Seymour knows the fragrance of hyacinths.' This may amount to knowing how to identify that fragrance, to name it and pick it out from other similar ones, but it doesn't seem at all to be a case of *knowing-that*.

And consider this example of case 3: 'Lucy knows how to whistle.' This sort of *knowing-how* appears to have nothing to do with any knowledge in senses 1 or 2 at all.

Almost all the philosophical tradition in epistemology concentrates on *knowing-that* – sense 1. Why this concentration? It has been claimed that it's the basic kind, and that other sorts of knowledge boil down to it – that is, that they can be understood wholly in terms of *knowing-that*. But you may find this implausible after having thought about all the different ways of knowing we've just mentioned. It could be, instead, that this is the most important kind of knowledge; but it's not clear why this might be so. Another possibility is that this kind of knowledge involves the most interesting puzzles and complexities. But the answer may be simply that the earliest philosophers chose this sort of knowledge to talk about and the later ones read them, and thought about what they said, and added their own thoughts, and so a tradition was set up of this sort of consideration, without any real reason for excluding other sorts.

Anyway, we'll follow the tradition by concentrating on *knowing-that*.

Knowing-that

Philosophers think of *knowing-that* as the kind of knowing whose object is a **proposition**. What's a proposition? Think of it as what a sentence means, what it expresses. So when two different sentences – sentences that differ in component words, or word order, or language – have the same meaning, they express the same proposition. So a single proposition is expressed by 'Fred loves Sally' and 'Sally is loved by Fred' and '*Fred liebt Sally.*'

Propositions are expressed by a whole declarative sentence, rather than, for example, just a noun or noun phrase. 'Fred loves Sally' is a declarative sentence, and expresses a proposition. When Marvin knows that Fred loves Sally, this proposition is the object of his knowledge. It's a case of knowing-that. 'Sally' and 'football' and 'who Sally is' and 'how to reach Sally by telephone' are not whole sentences – they're merely nouns or noun phrases. They do not express propositions. So when Marvin knows Sally or knows football, or knows who Sally is, or knows how to reach Sally by telephone, the object of his knowledge is not a proposition; these are not cases of knowing-that.

A noun is, roughly, a word that names something or a group of things: 'Arnold' and 'ducks' in 'Arnold is afraid of ducks.' A noun phrase is one or more words that function that way: 'Deciduous trees', 'their leaves', and 'autumn' in 'Deciduous trees drop their leaves in autumn.' A declarative sentence makes a statement, by contrast with, for example, 'Hello!' or 'Please pass the salt' or 'When's lunch?'

Another way to think about knowing with a propositional object is to notice that the object, the thing known, is something that's either true or false. If Fred loves Sally, the proposition expressed by the words 'Fred loves Sally' is true; if he doesn't, it's false. The contrast here is again with the other two senses of 'know', in which it doesn't make sense to say that what's said to be known is either true or false. Sally (whom Fred knows) is neither true nor false, and neither is football, or who Sally is, or how to reach Sally by telephone.

Sometimes we want to say that a declarative sentence expresses a fact. 'Christmas day occurred on Wednesday in 2002' expresses the fact that Christmas day occurred on Wednesday in 2002. 'It's raining in Peru' expresses the fact that it's raining in Peru – but only if that really is a fact. If it isn't raining in Peru, that sentence doesn't express a fact. Facts are never false. If a sentence is false, it doesn't express a fact. (It only purports to express a fact.) Because the object of supposed knowledge, what's said to be known, might be false, we say that the object is a proposition, not a fact.

Knowledge and truth

Now suppose that it's false that Fred loves Sally. That must make it false that Matilda knows that Fred loves Sally. If the propositional object is false, then any claim that somebody knows that propositional object must be false. This is just a matter of the conventional language use here. We don't say that something is known when we think it's false. To say that something is known is to imply that it's true. Of course, sometimes people say that they or somebody else knows something, but what's said to be known is false. That means that what they say is false. If Shirley said, 'Arnold knows that World War I ended in 1919', what Shirley says is false: Arnold doesn't know that, and you can tell Arnold doesn't know that without knowing anything about Arnold. (You don't even have to know who he is.) The reason is that the propositional object, that World War I ended in 1919, is false. It ended in 1918. So nobody can know that propositional object. Philosophers say: **Truth is a necessary condition for knowledge.** That means: if it ain't true, it ain't knowledge. Or, to use the letter abbreviations that philosophers are so fond of when they express a general formula: **The truth of p is a necessary condition for S knows that p.**

'Know' is thus what's called a *factive verb*. That means that the verb is used only when the speaker thinks that the embedded proposition is true. Other factive verbs are 'realize,' 'learn,' and 'remember'. You wouldn't say 'I remember that I went to the zoo on my fifth birthday' if you didn't think that you did go to the zoo on your fifth birthday.

Perhaps you have thought of this objection: it's not necessary for someone's *knowing something* that what they believe is true. We only expect that they've made a significant effort to find out that their belief is true. That is, their belief isn't just a prejudice, or a hunch, or a guess. That would make it merely a belief.

But there does seem to be a good reply to this analysis. Consider this example:

> Cynthia has made a very thorough and careful search of every room, and announces that she knows that her lost keys are nowhere in the house. Suddenly you notice her keys in a very unlikely spot, say underneath the refrigerator.

Would you still say that she *knew* that her keys were nowhere in the house? The answer seems to be *no*. She was entitled to say what she did; she did what she was supposed to do. She didn't jump to an unwarranted conclusion; she exercised due diligence in finding out the facts. But nevertheless, she didn't know that the keys were nowhere in the house, because what she believed (and claimed to know) was false. She didn't know what she said she knew. The distinction here is between two sorts of false belief: a false belief which just comes to you, a guess, without appropriate effort to determine its truth; and a false belief made after an appropriate and reasonable attempt to find out the truth. People who allow themselves the first sort of false claim are, in a way, failing to live up to their responsibilities, belief-wise; those who take more care with their beliefs are doing what they should. But either way, if a belief is false, it isn't knowledge.

Knowledge and belief

But if a belief is true, it doesn't follow that it's knowledge. Just because it's true that World War I ended in 1918, it doesn't follow that Arnold knows that World War I ended in 1918. Maybe Arnold doesn't know that because he doesn't even believe it. Maybe he believes it ended in 1919, not 1918, or maybe he doesn't have any beliefs at all about when World War I ended. Or maybe he's a product of today's educational system, and he's never heard of World War I, so he has no beliefs at all about it. In order for Arnold to know that p, he has to believe it. Philosophers say: **Belief is a necessary condition for**

knowledge; or *S believes that p* is a **necessary condition for** *S knows that p*.

The idea that knowledge involves belief is widely accepted among philosophers, but if you've had any experience with philosophy, you'll be aware that no matter how obvious and well-accepted something is, there'll be some philosophers who argue against it. That's the case here too.

The first argument we'll look at – briefly – involves examples such as this one:

> Abigail is very fond of her twin sister Aileen, but the sisters haven't seen each other for ten years, because Aileen has been working in a far-off country. It's Abigail's thirtieth birthday, and her friends have arranged that Aileen fly back for the occasion, and show up as a surprise in the middle of Abigail's party. As soon as Abigail realizes it's Aileen in front of her, she shrieks 'I don't believe it's really Aileen!' But she knows it's Aileen.

So is this knowledge without belief? Well, no. Abigail doesn't literally mean that she doesn't believe it's Aileen standing there. She of course *does* believe it's Aileen, and that's why she's shrieking with surprise. What she means by that exclamation is to indicate that she's really surprised.

Here's an objection that's slightly more serious. Consider this dialogue:

Donald: My science teacher Ms Schmidlap believes that biological species developed their characteristics through a process of evolution.

Daisy: What do you mean, '*believes*'? What Ms Schmidlap thinks is true. She doesn't *believe* it – she *knows* it.

This might suggest that knowledge is not a form of belief, but rather that they're different things: if you know something you don't believe it. But most philosophers would not agree with this diagnosis. What Daisy is saying in her reply to Donald is perhaps more precisely stated as 'No, she doesn't *just* believe it, she knows it.' The word 'just' here indicates that there's something more than mere belief here. When Daisy rejects the description of Ms Schmidlap's state as believing, she's following a kind of conversational rule that (roughly speaking) what you say should make the strongest claim available. So, for example, if someone asks you what you put in the basket, and you reply, 'I put a green apple in there', this is true when you put a green apple and a red apple and a pear in there. But somebody who noticed what you did might object that you put more than that in there. For you to make a weaker statement than you might have, with less information in it than was available to you, is rather misleading. It's a violation of this conversational rule, but it's not exactly false. Similarly, when Daisy rejects the description of Ms Schmidlap's state as belief, she's following the rule, rejecting a partial account for a fuller, stronger one. She's in effect correcting Donald's statement, on the basis that it hints that there's something less than knowledge there, because he doesn't describe it as such, but makes a weaker claim. It sounds like he's hinting that what Ms Schmidlap thinks isn't true, because he's not saying she knows it. But his weaker claim is nonetheless true. Not saying that a belief is true is not the same thing as saying that the belief is not true. So the dialogue, on this analysis, does not show that knowledge doesn't involve belief. It merely shows that knowledge involves belief and more. What more? We'll get to that in the next chapter.

2
Strength of belief and evidence

Strength of belief

Suppose Charlie hears the phone ring, and says, 'I believe that's Lucy phoning.' Then suppose he said instead, 'I know that's Lucy phoning.' Why say one rather than the other? What's the difference? What would lead Charlie to say that he knows p, rather than merely that he believes it?

You might say that Charlie believes that it's Lucy phoning, not that he knows it, because *you* think it's false that Lucy is on the phone. But that couldn't be the reason why Charlie would say one rather than the other. (He wouldn't say either that he knows it or that he believes it, if he thought it was false.)

Maybe the difference is the strength of Charlie's belief. We'd expect Charlie to say 'I believe it's Lucy phoning' when he sort of thinks it's Lucy phoning, but he wouldn't be willing to bet a whole lot of money on it. He thinks it's likely to be her, but he feels that he stands a chance of being wrong. He'd say 'I know that it's Lucy phoning' instead if he were very confident that it's Lucy phoning. In general, then, according to this suggestion, you say, 'I know' when your belief is quite strong, but 'I believe' when it's weaker. Maybe, then, we should add as a condition for the truth of S *knows that p* that S *is quite confident of p*: when S is less confident about p, S doesn't know that p. S merely believes that p. This might explain why Charlie said one of these rather than the other.

An influential, fairly recent analysis of knowledge is one by the English philosopher A. J. Ayer. He argues that 'being completely sure' is necessary for knowledge:

> It is indeed true that one is not reasonably said to know a fact unless one is completely sure of it. This is one of the distinctions between knowledge and belief ... But, whereas it is possible to believe what one is not completely sure of, so that one can consistently admit that what one believes to be true may nevertheless be false, this does not apply to knowledge.

A. J. Ayer (1910–89) was among the best known philosophers in Britain – a radio and TV personality, and a public champion of various political causes. He's known philosophically for his definitive statement of logical positivism, the doctrine that the meaning of any statement is nothing but the sense-experiences that would show that it's true; and that, consequently, a great deal of what's said in religion, ethics, and philosophy in general is without any meaning at all.

One thing you might find puzzling here is how Ayer can say that S cannot consistently claim to know something – that is, be sure of it – while admitting that p *may be* false. He argues that (just about) anything one believes has the logical possibility of being false; so everyone should admit that error is possible, no matter how sure of p. If you're really sure that p you feel that there's no *genuine* doubt, no *practical likelihood*, of your being wrong.

Is *strong* belief necessary?

To test this idea, we should examine cases in which S's belief is not strong, but it seems that he or she might be credited with knowledge anyway. Here's one:

Howard has memorized the capitals of all the countries of Europe in preparation for his school geography class. He gets nervous and full of self-doubt when he's called on in class to answer a question, and when his teacher asks him what the capital of Slovakia is, he feels like all that memorized information is evaporating. He hesitantly and doubtfully mumbles 'Bratislava?' His teacher asks, 'Do you believe that's the capital?' He replies, 'Well, yes, I guess so.' 'But,' continues the teacher, 'do you *know* that that's the capital?' He says, 'Well, er, no, not really.' In fact, he's got it right, and his belief is well founded: the source of his information is a reliable map he studied in the textbook, and his memory is good. He deserves to be sure that he's right – but he's not at all sure.

Does Howard *know* that the capital of Slovakia is Bratislava? Some philosophers agree with Ayer that he doesn't, and think that confidence is a necessary condition for knowledge. But others disagree, and would react to this story by saying that despite Howard's distrust of his memory, it really is working fine, and he knows what the capital is despite the fact that he thinks he doesn't.

The picture of knowledge given by this second point of view is that S's true belief that p counts as knowledge if S *should* feel sure about p – never mind whether S feels secure or not. Ayer thinks that *both* feeling secure *and* being entitled to feel secure are necessary. According to him, if you don't feel secure in a belief, then you don't know it; and even if you feel secure, if you don't deserve to feel secure, then you don't know it.

We can ask two questions here. First: is feeling secure really necessary? Then second: is deserving to be secure necessary? But this raises a third question: When do we deserve to feel secure in a belief? When, in other words, is a belief really *justified*?

Justification

What is justification? Well, this is a good question; various complicated answers have been proposed, and there is a good deal of controversy about which answer is right. We'll be working through these controversies as we proceed, but for the moment, you can think of the justification of a belief as what makes it reasonable to believe, what makes a belief secure. My justification for my belief that it's snowing out is that I've just looked out the window and seen the snow. For my belief that I sent Mildred an email this morning, that I remember doing it. For my belief that my sister just bought a new car, that she told me she did. For my belief that the Olympic bobsledding final is on TV tonight, that I read it in the newspaper. For Howard's belief that Bratislava is the capital of Slovakia, that his memory is trustworthy, and that he can remember that a reliable source of information told him this. For my belief that there exist giant clams that can weigh several hundred pounds – well, I don't remember what the basis for that belief was, but I think it must have been a reliable one.

You can see how strength of belief and strength of justification are closely connected. Ideally, the strength of someone's belief is closely correlated with how well justified that belief is. But sometimes it's not. Howard's belief is well justified but weak. More frequent, however (unfortunately), is belief that's strong but not well justified. Here are some examples of both kinds of mismatch:

> Darleen reads and believes her newspaper's daily horoscope column. She's always certain that the horoscope's predictions are correct – until they turn out clearly wrong (and then she makes excuses). So Darleen's justification for her belief that she's going to come into a lot of money later in the week is that it said so in her horoscope column. She thinks this is good justification for her belief, but it isn't.

Marvin has a very strong feeling that something terrible is going to go wrong today. In fact, this feeling is caused by a chemical problem in his brain, and has no justification. He knows he has no justification for this belief, and people tell him that he's just being crazy, but he can't shake the belief.

Archie has very good evidence that his wife is being unfaithful to him: he has seen copies of emails to her lover on their computer, credit card receipts from a motel, and so on. But Archie can't get himself to believe she's unfaithful. He recognizes that there is, in fact, some evidence there, but he just can't admit that it's conclusive. He has suspicions, but he doesn't feel sure. This is a case of very strong justification, but very weak belief (or no belief at all).

Susy's mum always told her to dress up warm on cold days, or else she'd catch a cold. She's heard this bit of folk-wisdom elsewhere too, and she believes it, because that's all she's ever heard about the subject. Medical research has conclusively proven, however, that dressing up warmly in cold weather has absolutely no effect on your probability of catching a cold. Susy's fairly firm belief is, in fact, unjustified.

Dr. Proctor is a scientist who has been investigating the causes of a mysterious disease. Her very careful and thorough experiments have satisfied all the scientific requirements for proof, but she won't say she's completely sure. She points out that there's always some possibility that science has made a mistake, no matter how good the evidence. She recommends this attitude as open-minded healthy scepticism.

Stanley is the most stubborn guy around. He latches onto a lunatic belief and nothing can dislodge it. The other day he just dreamed up the idea that mobile phone use is causing global warming. People try to reason with him, showing him that there's absolutely no evidence for this, and that the physics of mobile phone transmission and the dynamics of weather make this very implausible, but he's adamant.

What these examples show is that there are several independent questions that we might ask about S and his or her belief, when we're wondering whether S knows that p:

Does S believe p strongly?
Does S think he or she has justification?
Does what S thinks is justification really justify p strongly enough?
Is there strong justification for p that S doesn't have in mind?

Unshakable knowledge

The idea that strongly justified strong belief is a necessary condition for knowledge has had a good number of proponents in the history of philosophy. The most influential view of this sort was perhaps that of René Descartes. Speaking of the distinction between rigorous knowledge on the one hand, and mere ordinary conviction or belief on the other, Descartes writes:

> I distinguish the two as follows: there is conviction when there remains some reason which might lead us to doubt, but knowledge is conviction based on a reason so strong that it can never be shaken by any stronger reason.

He describes this sort of conviction as 'quite incapable of being destroyed … clearly the same as the most perfect certainty'.

René Descartes (1595–1650) was a French philosopher who is now thought of as the most important influence on modern (that is, post-Medieval) philosophy. He wrote extensively on epistemology, but he was also a very important physicist and mathematician. (You might remember that the method of graphing using vertical and horizontal origins uses what are called 'Cartesian coordinates' – this was invented by, and named after, Descartes.)

What exactly Descartes was aiming at here is a matter about which experts disagree. Perhaps he's thinking that knowledge has to be a belief that's *indubitable* or *incorrigible*, or *infallible*. These three terms need some explanation.

An **infallible** belief is one that cannot be wrong. If S believes p, then p must be true. It's impossible to falsely believe p. Sometimes philosophers use the terms 'indubitable' and 'incorrigible' as synonyms for 'infallible'. But sometimes they have a slightly different meaning. **Incorrigible** literally means *uncorrectable*, and some philosophers want to restrict its use to cases in which it's impossible for anyone other than S to have grounds for correcting S's belief. **Indubitable** literally means *undoubtable*: and to say that S's belief that p is indubitable is sometimes taken to mean that it's impossible for S to have grounds for rejecting it.

Incorrigibility and indubitability might be taken to be matters of strength of belief. A belief of S's might be so strong that nobody else would be able to shake it. Or so strong that nothing that S thought of, or that happened to S, would get S to revise that belief.

It's a matter of some controversy exactly how to understand what Descartes is claiming about the conditions for knowledge; but we might take him to be suggesting that all of these conditions are necessary for S to know that p:

p is true

S believes that p

S's belief is *psychologically* maximally strong – incorrigible and indubitable – that is, it's not psychologically possible for S to abandon belief in p

S's belief has these characteristics because S takes the justification for p to be so strong as to make the belief infallible – that is, it could not possibly be wrong

S is not being pigheaded or gullible: the belief that p really is infallible.

S's belief is indubitable and incorrigible because he or she thinks it's infallible, and it really is genuinely indubitable and incorrigible because it really is infallible. So the key element we'll examine right now is the requirement of infallibility of S's belief.

You can see that this requirement sets an extremely high standard – maybe too high – because if this is what's needed, then precious few of your everyday beliefs are really knowledge. Consider your belief that you had fried eggs for breakfast this morning. Is this infallible? That is, is it at all *possible* that this belief is mistaken? Let me convince you it is. Look, you've been mistaken once in a while about matters like this – perfectly obvious matters, which you observed very recently. Your observation and memory are normally quite trustworthy in matters like this, but rarely something goes wrong – maybe a little failure of attention or an unusual memory lapse. So this belief is not infallible. It's not very likely to be false – in fact, it's highly unlikely that you've got it wrong. But we're requiring *infallibility*, and this belief doesn't make the grade.

But then what belief would pass the requirement of infallibility? It's hard to think of any. Maybe there aren't any.

Suppose, then, that precious few of our ordinary beliefs pass this test, so they don't count as knowledge according to Descartes' criterion. What then? Here are three different responses one might have to this news:

1 I now see that knowledge is a much tighter concept than I thought, and that I've been mistakenly claiming I knew things all over the place when I really didn't. I guess I don't really know a lot of what I thought I did. I should re-examine what I thought I knew in this light, to see what if anything passes this very strict test.

2 No, look, the test you're proposing for what counts as knowledge rules out almost everything – maybe even everything – that people counted as knowledge, so you've got the

test for knowledge wrong. You're not talking about our concept of knowledge; you're talking about something else altogether. So you've given me no reason to change my claims to know things.

3   I agree that *very* strong justified confidence is a necessary condition for knowledge, but we shouldn't require such perfection. There's a vanishingly small possibility I'm wrong about various obvious things we know. We should have a more reasonable test for the sort of certainty required here. We shouldn't require complete infallibility. We should require a less stringent sort of certainty.

Descartes would endorse 1, but he might be somewhat sympathetic to 2 as well. There's some reason to interpret his analysis as applying to a special kind of knowledge, a special sense of the word 'knowledge', not one that people ordinarily talk about. Sometimes translators and commentators present him as talking about *rigorous knowledge*, or *scientific knowledge*, which might reasonably be thought to have a higher standard for certainty than the ordinary garden-variety. It might still be the case, however, that his standard is so high that it can't be met even by our best attempts to be rigorous or scientific. What if we softened that requirement?

Descartes argued that the beliefs that arise from one's ordinary everyday sense-experience weren't infallible. There's always the possibility that our senses are playing tricks on us (he imagined a malevolent demon who gives us hallucinations), or that we're dreaming. He concluded that sense-experience could not provide the kind of genuine knowledge he was interested in. But he added that we needn't worry that *all* our everyday experiences are hallucinations, because God wouldn't provide us with senses and then let them be totally useless. But we have to be aware of their limitations, and seek genuine infallible knowledge elsewhere.

Indubitability and incorrigibility without infallibility

Suppose, then, that we drop perfect infallibility as a requirement for knowledge, but hold on to the idea that knowledge must be a very strong kind of belief – a belief that's indubitable and incorrigible in some way, even though not infallible. Is this a possible way to think about things? Can there be indubitability and incorrigibility without infallibility? Or does fallibility of a belief imply that it's corrigible (that is that it's possible that someone would show you you're wrong about it)? And does it imply that it's dubitable (that is, does it raise doubts about that belief, and make it possible for you to change your mind)?

It's possible, of course, for a belief of S's to be fallible, but nevertheless incorrigible and indubitable for S, because S is merely pig-headedly stubborn about believing p. If someone gave S good reasons that made it reasonable to think that p was false, or if S him- or herself encountered these, he or she'd just refuse to reconsider. Nothing that S could encounter could show S that p is false, or even raise any doubt in S's mind about p. So for S, p is indubitable. Nobody else could possibly show S that p is false, so for S, p is incorrigible.

If we're going to make these two features of belief require-ments for knowledge, it wouldn't be proper to let them be satis-fied by S because of his or her irrational stubbornness. What we're looking for is an account of incorrigibility and indubitabil-ity that doesn't depend on either irrationality or infallibility. Is there any such account? Some philosophers have argued that there are genuine cases in which it's rational to be completely sure of something, in which one's belief is incorrigible and indubitable though fallible, and this is not mere stubbornness, but is instead good belief practice.

Here's one way a belief might be thought to satisfy these requirements. Consider again your belief about your breakfast.

You've admitted that it's fallible. But does that raise any possibility of your changing your mind about it? Let's be careful here: it's one thing to admit that there's a very tiny possibility that the belief is false, but this is consistent with there being no possibility at all that you change your mind about it. Here's how this might be rational. You have an extremely strong justification for that belief: you remember breakfast very clearly, and your memory is almost always reliable about the obvious features of very recent events you've experienced. To make you change your mind about this belief, or even to raise any doubt that it's correct, you'd need some counter-evidence that's stronger than what you've got in its favour. But your current evidence is so strong that you'd conclude that any possible counter-evidence was misleading. For example, if your mum insisted that you had cereal for breakfast, you'd decide that *she* had somehow dreamed it, or was suffering a peculiar memory breakdown, or something, before you'd even begin to doubt your own memory about something so recent and obvious. The same sort of thing applies to beliefs you have based on immediate clear sense-perception, under ideal conditions, of ordinary objects. You can see that there's a coffee-cup on the table, and the light is good, and so is your eyesight, and you haven't been taking any illegal drugs, so *any* evidence that you're mistaken would be insufficient to raise any doubts. There's a tiny possibility you really are mistaken – it's not an infallible belief – but no possibility of doubt.

The point is, here, that when S believes p, and has justification for that belief, but is confronted with evidence against p, there are two possibilities: S might either take that counter-evidence seriously and doubt or reject p, or else hold on to that belief that p, and doubt or reject the counter-evidence. Sometimes the first approach is the rational one; somebody who never acted that way is irrational, stubborn, pig-headed. But sometimes, the second course of action is the rational one. In these cases, even though the belief is fallible, and S knows it's fallible, what we have here is rational incorrigibility and indubitability.

The advantage of this approach is that it's implausible to think that there's any kind of belief that guarantees its own infallibility. Ayer claims, plausibly, that it never follows from the fact that someone believes something that it's true. Even when that person believes it with maximum strength.

3
Justification and Gettier problems

Ayer's position that we were looking at in the last chapter is that some true beliefs, even some that are maximally strong, don't count as knowledge; what's needed, in addition, is that the believer is entitled to hold that belief. A belief that's just a hunch or a guess doesn't carry with it a great likelihood of being true, no matter how strongly it's held. It might be true, of course; but if it is true we wouldn't call it *knowledge*, because the believer didn't have an adequate basis for that belief. Philosophers usually speak of this requirement for knowledge as the necessity for **justification** of the belief. So it has become the view of many epistemologists that knowledge is justified true belief.

What justification is, exactly, turns out to be a very controversial matter. Is it a matter of what you believe or what you experience? Are there basic beliefs which justify others but are themselves unjustified? Can you have justification you're not aware of? Are there things you know (or don't know) or things that have to be true (or not) that produce or interfere with justification? It's even controversial whether justification is actually required for knowledge. We're going to be looking at a variety of problems for the idea of justification, at some theories of what justification is, and some alternatives to the view that it's necessary. We'll start by looking at some very important objections to the idea that knowledge is true belief which is (in some simple way) justified.

A Gettier example

For a long time, philosophers were convinced that they knew what justification was, and that this was a necessary feature of knowledge. But a two-page paper published in 1963 by Edmund Gettier (American philosopher, born 1927) revolutionized the philosophical study of knowledge by convincing just about everyone that knowledge could not be simply justified true belief. All that paper did was to present a couple of examples to show that the traditional account (he specifically mentioned Ayer) was inadequate.

To understand Gettier's reasoning, you'll need a tiny bit of background about his two assumptions. The first one, in Gettier's words, is that beliefs *entailed* by other justified beliefs are themselves justified.

> Saying that a statement p **entails** another q is to say that if p were true, then q would also have to be true – in other words, that it's impossible that p be true, but q false. So, for example, 'The test is on Tuesday' entails 'The test is on Tuesday or it's on Wednesday.' If the first statement is true, the second would have to be true also. We can also speak of a set of statements {p, q, ...} entailing another, s: that means that if all the statements in the set are true, then s would have to be true also. So, for example, the set of two statements {'If it's Tuesday, then the exam is today', and 'It's Tuesday'} entails 'The exam is today.' Another way of saying the same thing is that the first statement (or set of statements) *logically implies* the other one.

This first assumption seems obviously true. If you're justified in thinking that all Marvin's sisters are older than he is, and that Melissa is Marvin's sister, then clearly you're justified in thinking that Melissa is older than Marvin. If you're justified in thinking that the test is on Tuesday, then it must be that you're also justified in thinking that the test is on Tuesday or it's on Wednesday.

Gettier's second assumption is that one can be justified in believing a proposition that's false. This sounds reasonable. Think of court cases with plenty of good evidence that the innocent accused is guilty. This unfortunately happens.

Here is an example that has the same point as one of Gettier's (but is a story that's a little more plausible):

> Joan believes that if either of her enemies Jack or Jim was appointed new office supervisor, there'd be a letter in her mailbox telling her that she's fired. The office gossip, who is usually a very reliable source of information, tells Joan that Jack got the job. So Joan concludes that a letter firing her is in her mailbox. She's right about the letter, but it's because her enemy Jim got the job.

Let's get straight what's happening here. Joan believes, with justification (we assume):

Statement A: 'Jack got the job.' and
Statement B: 'If Jack or Jim got the job, there would be a letter in her mailbox firing her.'

Statement A is justified and false, but according to Gettier's second assumption, a false belief may be justified. Note that those two statements A and B entail:

Statement C: 'There's a letter in her mailbox firing her.'

Statement C is true. Now, according to Gettier's first assumption, because A and B are both justified, and they together entail C, therefore C is justified. So: C is justified, and true, and Joan believes it. If knowledge is simply justified true belief, then Joan knows that C. But this is clearly wrong. Joan doesn't know C; and most philosophers would say she doesn't. Given that, there must be something wrong either with one or the other of Gettier's assumptions, or with the idea that knowledge is simply justified true belief. He concludes that knowledge is not simply justified true belief.

Ayer's response to Gettier

Ayer recognized that this sort of Gettier example posed a problem for his account. His response in defence of his account was that one of Gettier's assumptions, the first one listed above, was wrong. It's not true that just any logical deduction from justified propositions was itself justified. He would say, then, that while Joan's belief that Jack got the job was justified but false (and her belief that if Jack or Jim got the job, there'd be a letter in her mailbox firing her was also justified), what they entailed was not justified.

What's needed here, Ayer argued, was a more careful account of what justification involved – one that showed why it was not necessarily carried over from any justified beliefs to what those beliefs entailed. Of course, you can't just say that justification is what you have when a true belief is in fact knowledge – that would simply be circular. It would be no easy job to specify independently of this exactly what was needed here, Ayer admitted, but he pointed out that this sort of problem was not news: well before Gettier, Carl Hempel had pointed out problems with the notion of *evidence for p* that were exactly the sort that Gettier was illustrating here.

Ayer is no doubt correct that it would be nice if the notion of justification were carefully explained in such a way as to eliminate this problem. But his advice doesn't seem to take care of examples close enough to the ones provided by Gettier to be known as 'Gettier cases'.

Carl Hempel, German-American philosopher (1905–97) proposed around 1940, but did not solve, what's called the **Raven Paradox**. Here's how it goes. The statement, 'All ravens are black' is logically equivalent to the statement 'Everything that is not black is not a raven.' Each statement entails the other. So, it seems, what's evidence for one should be evidence for the other. Examination of something that's not black, like one of my pink socks, which turns out not to be a raven, provides a little evidence for 'Everything that's not black is not a raven.' Just a very little evidence, but some. But, it seems, examination of that sock provides no evidence at all – not even a little – for the statement 'All ravens are black.' I'll make this clear.

Let's abbreviate these statements:

E: My non-black sock is not a raven.
s: Everything that's not black is not a raven.
t: All ravens are black.

And this is the situation:

E is evidence for statement s.
Statement s logically implies statement t.
If x entails y, then what's evidence for x should be evidence for y.
But E is no evidence at all for statement t.

This Raven Paradox has generated a lot of philosophical literature attempting to elucidate the notion of evidence, to specify when the relation *x is evidence for y* may be transferred to *x is evidence for z*. This, however, is a very difficult problem. Ayer's point is that the Gettier problem is just the same problem all over again, and might be solved with a similar (and similarly difficult) elucidation of when *x is justified* may be transferred to *y is justified*.

Here's one:

> Max sees what are, in fact, two very realistic decoy ducks on the lake, and he takes them to be real ducks. Max's belief that there are ducks on the lake is well justified, because he's very good, in general, at duck-recognition; and it's true, because there are in fact ducks on the lake – on the other side, where he didn't see them.

But Max doesn't know there are ducks on the lake. There isn't any inference here of the sort that occurs in the Jack/Jim case. Ayer's suggestion doesn't help with this example because no problem arises concerning the transfer of justification between a statement and what it implies.

The no-falsehood reply

It may have occurred to you that the reason we don't want to count Joan's belief as knowledge is that she comes to it by reasoning from a false premise – that Jack will get the job. She's just lucky that her conclusion from this premise and her other knowledge – that both enemies would fire her with a letter in her mailbox – turns out to be true. Suppose then that we specify, as a condition for knowledge, that S has justified true belief *based on no false premises*. This is the **no-falsehood reply**.

But the example involving Max, above, might be taken to show that this requirement won't work either. Max, it seems, is not reasoning from any false premise. He doesn't appear to be reasoning at all. He just had the visual experience he did, and immediately, with no reasoning intervening, came to his belief.

But defenders of the no-falsehood reply have a counter-argument here. They might say that despite appearances, Max *is* reasoning, and his reasoning does have a false premise. Here's how we might reconstruct Max's reasoning:

1   That looks like some ducks on the lake.
2   I'm a pretty good identifier of ducks, under good conditions
    for observation.
3   Conditions for observation are good.
4   So I'm not being deceived now.
5   Therefore there are ducks on the lake.

And step 4 of this is false.

Of course, Max probably isn't thinking propositions 1 through 4 when he sees what he sees, and begins to believe proposition 5; but it's questionable whether we should restrict S's beliefs and reasoning to what S is actually thinking about. You believed a minute ago that they grow coffee beans in South America, though it's unlikely you were actually thinking about this. You hear the doorbell ring, so you immediately think it's Matilda come to visit; maybe the best way to understand this is that you're going through a reasoning process – that the doorbell means there's someone there, that Matilda is more likely to visit right now than anyone else – though these aren't conscious thoughts.

But on the other hand it's not at all clear that we should treat this sort of belief that comes so immediately, without conscious inference anyway, as a case of inference – of reasoning – at all. But, just to see where this line of argument leads, let's accept it for the moment. The proposal is, then, that a necessary condition for *S knows that p* is that S does not arrive at that belief from a false premise.

Problems with the no-falsehood reply

But requiring the truth of *every* belief that may have figured somehow, unconsciously, in Max's current belief appears to be much too strong a condition: it rules out all sorts of things we ordinarily count as knowledge. After all, we all suffer from all sorts of (usually unimportant) false beliefs that figure in our cognitive processes. For example:

> Mildred believes that it sometimes snows in May where she lives. (And she's right.) In support of this, she can tell you about the time it was snowing on the day in May 1993 when she flew back from sunny Aruba. Well, she's wrong about this. It did snow on the day in May 1993 when she returned, but she was coming back from sunny Antigua, not sunny Aruba.

But that doesn't mean that Mildred doesn't know that it sometimes snows in May where she lives. In this case, it doesn't matter that this particular bit of support for her belief is false. It's clearly knowledge anyway. What we want, instead, is to rule out cases (like Max's) in which there's a false belief that's an *important* part of S's justification.

So maybe what we need here is a way to sort out the important parts of S's justification for believing p from the unimportant parts. One proposal here is that an unimportant part is one such that, had it been eliminated from the evidence, the case for p would still be as good – or would, in any case not have been considerably weaker.

Had the belief that she was coming back from Aruba been eliminated from Mildred's reasoning, her justification for her belief about snowing would not have been weakened even slightly. But cases in which the justification is weakened to some extent pose more of a problem. How much is 'considerably'? Consider this case:

> Albert has checked out the fruit bins at the supermarket every time he's been there this summer; all but one time, he's seen that the mangos are unripe. That other time, he in fact checked out unripe papayas (not being able to tell them from mangoes), though the mangoes in fact were unripe then too. From his

large number of beliefs that he saw unripe mangos, he concludes that it's very unlikely to find ripe mangoes there in the summer. He's correct, and he's got very good evidence for it.

That single false belief which is part of the basis for his conclusion does not make his belief unjustified, so it's not thus disqualified from being knowledge. But suppose that ten per cent of the time he looked at the papayas instead. Or fifty per cent or seventy-five per cent. The evidence gets weaker and weaker as the number of misidentifications increases. How weak does it have to be before we can deny that Albert has knowledge? For this proposal to be workable, it seems that some sort of answer needs to be given to this (perhaps unanswerable) question. **Vagueness** – the problem of where to draw a line – is of course a widespread problem elsewhere.

An additional problem, probably more serious, is illustrated by this story:

Larry believes Lulu will phone this evening, because she promised to, and she's very reliable. She picks up her cordless telephone to call, but there's something wrong with it and it doesn't work. But then she remembers that she has an old plug-in extension telephone in the attic; so she gets this down, plugs it in, and calls Larry.

Suppose Larry's conclusion that Lulu will phone is based on these other beliefs:

BELIEF 1: Lulu promised to phone.
BELIEF 2: She's very reliable.

His conclusion is well justified, and it turns out to be true; it's a clear and simple case of ordinary knowledge.

But suppose that Larry also believed that Lulu's regular phone was working. Now his justification for his conclusion includes these beliefs:

BELIEF 1: Lulu promised to phone.
BELIEF 2: She's very reliable.
BELIEF 3: Her (regular) telephone is working.

Belief 3 is false, so the no-falsehood reply would presumably judge that Larry didn't know she would call.

But suppose that, in addition, Larry believed that she had an old but usable spare telephone in the attic. Now he believes:

BELIEF 1: Lulu promised to phone.
BELIEF 2: She's very reliable.
BELIEF 3: Her (regular) telephone is working.
BELIEF 4: She has a spare working phone in the attic.

The addition of (true) belief 4 to the other three would make the false belief 3 unimportant, because if he had the opposite of belief 3, he would still be quite justified in his conclusion on the basis of beliefs 1, 2, and 4. Let's call belief 4 a 'fixer' belief: what it does is accommodate the falsehood of another belief, so that the conclusion follows after all; the false belief doesn't matter. According to the current addition to the no-falsehood reply, you can still have knowledge if your belief is based on a false belief, provided that you have this 'fixer' belief for the falsehood. So given the proviso added to the no-falsehood reply above, if Larry had these four beliefs, he would know that Lulu would call.

But belief 4 is (given belief 1, 2, and 3) completely gratuitous: it doesn't figure in Larry's reasoning at all. (Remember: he doesn't know – doesn't even consider – the possibility that her regular phone is broken.) Nevertheless, according to the no-falsehood reply, without this belief his conclusion isn't knowledge, but if he just happens to have it, then it is knowledge. This is a very odd consequence. It means that in order for you to have knowledge in any particular case, you must have 'fixer' beliefs – beliefs which you don't even consider – for anything false in your justification. Things that are furthest from your mind, then, may be relevant to whether or not you have knowledge in any particular case.

The no-defeaters reply

As we've seen, a worrying feature of the no-falsehood reply is that it presupposes that there are all sorts of 'unconscious' beliefs that are sources of S's justification for p, but which S is totally unaware of – perhaps could never become aware of.

A popular sort of reply to Gettier that's somewhat like the no-falsehood reply does not need this assumption. It's called the **'no-defeaters reply'**. A 'defeater' is a true proposition that S does not know, but that would have undermined S's evidence for p. In the Max-and-the-ducks example, for instance, this proposition is that what Max sees is decoy ducks.

The difference between this and the no-falsehood reply is that in the latter, we have to understand Gettier cases as ones in which S's justification is undermined by a false belief of S's, that's importantly involved in that justification. In this reply, it's not thought that S necessarily believes anything false; it's just that S hasn't (maybe even couldn't) take into account all the facts, at least one of which would have undermined S's belief.

Note carefully that unlike the other responses to Gettier we've looked at, the no-defeaters reply does not try to fix up the notion of justification; instead it proposes a different condition for knowledge altogether. The no-defeaters reply couldn't be a condition for justification, because, as we've seen, it's possible that a false belief could be justified; but for every false belief there's always a defeater – a true proposition that undermines S's evidence for p – the proposition that not-p *itself*. What we're interested in here is not the justification condition, but rather an additional condition.

So according to this position, S knows that p provided that S believes that p and p is true and justified, and, in addition, there is no true proposition that would undermine S's justification had he or she known it.

This seems to work well on some cases. If Joan had known that what the office gossip had told her was false, and that Jack didn't get the job, this would have undermined her justification for the belief that there'd be that letter in her mailbox. There is a defeater here, so Joan does not know that there was that letter in her mailbox. In the Max-and-the-ducks case, there also is a defeater: the fact that there were a number of decoy ducks there. Max was unaware of this fact, but had he been aware of it, it would have undermined his justification for believing that there were ducks on the lake, because he would think that maybe what he saw were decoys. So he doesn't know there are ducks on the lake. The true proposition Mildred doesn't know is that she was coming back from Antigua, not Aruba; but this is not a defeater, because it wouldn't have undermined her justification for the conclusion, which she really does know. All these cases get correct results when we apply the no-defeaters proposal.

Problems with the no-defeaters reply

One problem that this reply appears to share with the no-falsehood reply is vagueness. There are facts that don't completely undermine the justification for p — just reduce it considerably. The fact that there were only two decoys among hundreds of ducks on the lake would reduce Max's justification only a very little bit, not enough to deny him knowledge. (But the fact that what he saw were these two decoys would be enough.) So we would need to have some explanation of how we're to tell how much potential justification reduction is required to rule out a belief as knowledge.

But a different sort of objection is posed by this counter-example:

> Stu believes (correctly, and with excellent justification) that Pru is on her way and will arrive at his house in five minutes. By coincidence, the phone will ring at exactly the same instant Pru rings the doorbell, so Stu won't hear it. Had he believed the true proposition that he won't hear the doorbell in five minutes, his justification for his belief about Pru's arrival would have been undermined.

The true proposition that Stu will not hear the doorbell is a defeater, but in this case, it seems clear, Stu *does* know that Pru will arrive in five minutes. So the presence of a defeater does not mean there's no knowledge.

Another example that provides an objection to the no-defeaters proposal is the Larry-and-Lulu case – an example that also meant trouble for the no-falsehoods reply. Consider Larry in the simple state of merely believing that Lulu would call because she promised she would and she's reliable. (No beliefs about the phone's working or the spare.) The facts assumed in this case do include a defeater: that Lulu's phone isn't working. Had Larry believed this, the justification for his conclusion would have been considerably reduced – so the no-defeaters response tells us that even in that simple state Larry does not have knowledge. This is a different result from the one we assumed when considering the no-falsehoods reply. Who is right about this case? Does Larry in this simple state have knowledge or not? If your intuitions are that Larry does know that Lulu will call, you'd have to reject the no-defeaters reply, at least as we've been considering it.

Here's a possible reply to this objection. The intuition is correct that Larry does know, but we can fix the no-defeaters reply so that it agrees with this. Suppose we change it to make the necessary additional condition for knowledge not that there are no defeaters, but rather that there are no *undefeated defeaters*. In the Larry/Lulu case, the potential defeater, that Lulu's phone isn't working, is itself defeated by another fact, that she has a working spare. So if Larry had happened to know all of this, then he would be justified in his conclusion.

But this reply gets us into more problems. What this would mean is that merely determining that there's a defeater would not be sufficient for denying that there's knowledge. We'd also have to determine that no defeater for that defeater exists; it seems that we'd have to survey *all the facts of the case*, whatever this means. But this sort of demand for omniscience was already a problem for the simpler no-defeaters reply: if all we had to do was find out simply that a justified belief had no defeaters, wouldn't that already necessitate a survey of all the facts?

What's coming

We haven't finished with attempts to create adequate necessary and sufficient conditions for knowledge – attempts to deal with (more and more sophisticated) Gettier-type examples. So far, we've considered some attempts to patch up (or replace) the notion of justification to allow it to survive Gettier and Gettier-type counter-examples. But problems have been found with all of them. In the next chapter we'll consider instead some larger-scale theories of knowledge which attempt to deal with counter-examples, of course, but, in a larger sense, to accord more with our intuitive sense of what knowledge really is.

4

Internalism, externalism, and justification

In the last chapter, we surveyed a few attempts to patch up the traditional account of knowledge as justified true belief where it fell prey to Gettier-type (and other) counter-examples. In this chapter, we'll consider two post-Gettier attempts to rethink what knowledge is in larger scale ways.

What has always been clear to philosophers, pre- and post-Gettier, is that true belief is not sufficient, all by itself, for knowledge. Your true belief, after all, might just be a lucky guess, or a mere coincidence. What you know, by contrast, couldn't be just this. It must be more reliable, something we could *count on* to some extent to provide true belief. The idea that true belief needs to be *justified* was a way to add the ingredient that seemed necessary.

Philosophers' attempts to add this component to the requirements for knowledge can be sorted into two types. The first takes the question 'What is knowledge?' to be asking what a person has to do to achieve knowledge – what's going on in me when I've got it. The second takes that question to ask, rather, about what sort of facts about the world (including me) must be the case when I have knowledge. Theories that try to answer the knowledge-question understood in the first way are called **internalist** theories, because they concentrate on the 'internal' state of the knower. Those that try to answer the question understood in the second way are called **externalist** theories.

For a quick view of the difference between these two, let's return to Ayer and Descartes.

Descartes, you'll recall, demands infallibility for genuine knowledge. What sort of belief will have this feature? Not those that we get from the senses, but rather those that arise as a result of what he calls 'intuition'.

> By intuition I understand, not the fluctuating testimony of the senses, nor the misleading judgment that proceeds from the blundering constructions of imagination, but the conception which an unclouded and attentive mind gives us so readily and distinctly that we are wholly freed from doubt about that which we understand.

These beliefs will be distinguished from unreliable ones by the fact that they are 'clear and distinct':

> I call 'clear' that perception which is present and manifest to an attentive mind: just as we say that we clearly see those things which are present to our intent eye and act upon it sufficiently strongly and manifestly. On the other hand, I call 'distinct', that perception which, while clear, is so separated and delineated from all others that it contains absolutely nothing except what is clear.

There has been a lot of philosophical work done trying to produce an account of exactly what Descartes meant here, and of why that sort of belief might be considered infallible. You can possibly get a feeling for what he means when you consider the basic truths of arithmetic, or the 'self-evident' axioms of geometry. But what we're interested in at the moment is just that this is clearly an internalist view of the criteria for knowledge. Knowledge needs to be infallible belief, that kind of belief can be recognized by the mental operations we go through to get and understand these beliefs. So the justification Descartes demands for genuine knowledge is accomplished when we examine the source of a belief, and discover that the mental operations necessary for knowledge have been accomplished.

For Descartes, then, when you know that p, you can always give your justification (by demonstrating, somehow, the clarity and distinctness of your thought that p); and you thus always know that you know p. The position that in order to know that p, S must have 'access' to what justifies that belief, is an important form of epistemological internalism. We'll call it **access internalism**.

> Access internalists sometimes argue for what's called the **KK-thesis**: that whenever S knows that p, S knows that he or she knows that p. ('KK' abbreviates 'Know-Know'.) Philosophers unhappy with this argue that it follows from the KK-thesis that if S knows that he/she knows that p, then S must know that he/she knows that he/she knows that p – and so on, leading to an infinite regress, and thus requiring, for each bit of genuine knowledge, an infinite number of other bits.

Ayer agrees with Descartes that justification is required for knowledge. The way he puts it is that merely being completely sure is not enough: in addition, one must have *the right to be* completely sure.

A place where he disagrees with Descartes, however, is about the sense in which one must *have* justification. Descartes (implicitly) and other philosophers (more explicitly) demand that one be aware of the justifying factors for one's belief, and (perhaps) even that one be aware that they constitute justification. But Ayer's requirement is weaker: simply that you have sufficient justification, whether you know what this justification is or not.

Ayer remarks that ordinarily when someone is asked 'How do you know?' the reply will be forthcoming. But he's willing to grant S knowledge that p even when S can't say how he or she knows, provided that the source of S's belief entitles him or her to believe it. Ayer produces an example like this one:

> Noreen is consistently successful in predicting, before the season starts, which team will win the World Cup. Even real sports experts can't reliably predict this, and Noreen doesn't know how she does it.

Ayer says that a consistently good record at predicting might induce us to say that Noreen knew what team was going to win. Ayer would allow this even if S's predictions were of events that we'd consider unpredictable – earthquakes, for example – or even random, like lotteries; and even if nobody can figure out how S is doing it. He admits that this *appears* to dissolve the difference between knowing that p, and just making a lucky guess. It seems like a series of lucky guesses to Noreen and to the rest of us. The only reason to think any differently is that Noreen is so consistently good at her predictions, that we'd have to grant her the right to be certain. We concede this because we think that there is some justification for her belief – how else could she be consistently right? – though nobody has any idea what it is.

Ayer's case is fictitious and, of course, very implausible. But there are real-life examples rather like this – for example, chicken-sexers. These are people who can sort out male and female chicks when they're freshly hatched, rapidly and very accurately, after a glance at the chick's rear end. At this stage, long before the obvious external differences between hens and roosters have developed, there appears to be no external difference between the two sexes; and chicken-sexers usually say that they can't say how they sort the chicks out: the chicks *just look* male or female to them. In Ayer's case, nobody has a clue how Noreen does it, but chicken-sexers clearly do it by visual cues. But there's still a mystery here: they can't say what these cues are, what justifies their belief about the chick's sex.

For Ayer, then, justification gives the right to be sure – as it does for Descartes – and this right is granted by some mechanism that produces reliably true belief; but the difference is that for Ayer, this mechanism is not necessarily one that the believer is aware of. It can work without any representation in S's conscious mind. Thus Ayer denies access internalism; he is an externalist about justification.

Access internalism without actual awareness

Access internalism holds that a necessary condition for knowledge is that one has access to one's evidence. But it is clear that requiring that one be *aware* of one's justification for p whenever one knows that p is too strong. Consider this example:

> Barbie believes it's been snowing, despite having been in a windowless office all day. She thinks about that when getting ready to leave at 5, realizing that the snow might mean it will take her a little longer to get home. What she doesn't think about at 5 is her justification for her belief that it was snowing: having seen Ken come into the office with snowy boots on.

Barbie's true belief at 5 is justified by her earlier having seen Ken's snowy arrival, but she doesn't think about that at 5. We'd say that she knows at 5 that it's been snowing nevertheless. An internalist should insist that Barbie's belief does have an internal justification arising from her earlier experience anyway: she knows at 5 that snowy Ken arrived earlier, and that this is why she believes at 5 that it was snowing; but she's not thinking about it just then.

Of course there are things you believe at times you're not thinking about them. You believed a second ago that they grow coffee in Brazil, though your conscious thoughts were no doubt entirely elsewhere. What shows that you believed this was that you could have called this belief to mind if circumstances warranted it – if, for example, someone asked you whether they grow coffee there.

So we might amend the internalist view to say that a true belief is knowledge when it is justified by another belief – one that S is aware of, or could be aware of by reflecting on the matter. Thus we'd expect Barbie to be able to tell us how she knows it's snowing, if asked. If she weren't able to tell us, then it wouldn't be knowledge – or so the internalist might claim.

But now consider this slightly changed example:

> At 5, Barbie believes it's been snowing, despite having been in a windowless office all day. She's seen three people come into the office with snow on their boots. Ken was the first to come in, at 4, and his arrival with snowy boots was in fact her reason for believing it had been snowing. When Jill and Jack came in with snow on their boots at 4:15, she already knew it had been snowing. Now Pierre asks her how she knew that it has been snowing. She remembers, on reflection, having seen Ken, Jill, and Jack come in with snow on their boots, but she can't remember which one came in first, and was thus the basis of her belief.

Barbie is aware of what in fact was the source of her belief (Ken's snowy arrival), but she's not aware *that it was* the source of her belief. Is her awareness – her memory – of this event enough to give her knowledge? Some philosophers might say no. Plato, for example, decided that S doesn't genuinely know p if S can't give an account of the basis of this knowledge. In this case, he might judge that Barbie can't give enough of an account. But, Plato's view of what constitutes knowledge might well be counted as overly strict.

In any event, we might wonder whether it's even necessary that Barbie remember the event when she reflects on the matter.

Suppose that when Pierre asks, she thinks about it for a minute, and can't come up with any idea how she knows it's snowing. But later she happens to see the video surveillance tape from this morning, showing Ken's entrance, and her remarking to him that she can certainly see that it's been snowing, and then she remembers. Is this prompted awareness enough? Or suppose she still doesn't remember, and nothing can prompt her to, but she infers from that video tape what happened, and what in fact the basis for her belief was. So in a sense then she becomes aware of the basis. Is this enough?

But suppose now that nothing can ever prompt her to think about her evidence. She saw Ken come in, and this justified the belief that it had been snowing, and this belief simply stayed with her after she forgot all about Ken's arrival, permanently.

I'll bet you believe that 32 degrees Fahrenheit is the freezing point of water, that the Eiffel Tower is in Paris, that chickens lay eggs, that Jupiter is bigger than Mars, and on and on, but that you can't remember how you found any of this out, and will never – in any sense – be able to remember. All this, it seems, pretty clearly, is knowledge. This points to the externalist view, that all that's necessary for true belief to be knowledge is that S has a good basis for believing p, not that S knows or can become aware of what that basis is.

The deontological account of justification

A second way that knowledge can be seen to have necessary internalist conditions is by thinking of success at justification of a belief as a matter internal to the believer – a matter not of what facts are out there, but of how diligently the believer acted to make sure the belief in question accorded with the facts.

The idea here is that you have certain responsibilities as an epistemic agent – as someone who has beliefs. You're not living up to those responsibilities when you believe things without appropriate investigation into whether they're really true. Calling S's belief that p 'knowledge', then, is not just saying that p is true; it also praises S for having gone through the appropriate actions involved in seeking justification for p.

This sort of approach to knowledge emphasizes its **normative** nature. A 'normative' system is one that includes standards, one that tells us not just what is the case, but what ought to be the case. It tells us what we should be doing, what we're permitted to do and not permitted to do. To say that epistemology is normative, then, is to say that it systematically reveals the standards for proper belief formation – standards that we, as knowers, are supposed to follow.

There is a clear analogy here with ethics, which is much more obviously normative. Ethically speaking, S may or may not be justified in doing an action, and it's S's responsibility to try to make sure of doing only what is justified – to do what one must, and to avoid what one must not do. In epistemology, similarly, there are actions that are justified and those that are not: but in this case, all the relevant actions are beliefs.

This notion of justification – conceiving it as a matter of following one's epistemic obligations – is known as the **deonto-logical view** of justification.

The word 'deontological' has its home in philosophical ethics, where it refers to the view that the rightness or wrongness of actions is a matter of whether the person who did them tried to act in accordance with moral duty, even if the act has bad results. The analogy here is that epistemological deontology considers S's *believing that p* with regard to whether or not S tried to act in accordance with epistemological duty, by trying to assure that there was enough good reason to believe p.

Consider this example.

Alice is wondering, on Sunday, whether Zeke will arrive the next day. She remembers that he told her several weeks ago that he would arrive on Monday. She also recalls that he's been very trustworthy about such things in the past. She thinks: Is there anything else relevant I haven't considered? She decides there isn't, and concludes he'll arrive tomorrow. But Zeke's car has broken down en route, and he won't show up on Monday. He's stranded in the middle of nowhere, and can't call to tell her, so Alice doesn't know about Zeke's problem, and there's no way she could know about it.

Would you say that Alice has fulfilled her epistemic responsibilities? It seems so. Her belief is false – he won't arrive on Monday – and of course, she doesn't know that he'll arrive on Monday. But that's not the issue. The issue is whether she's done all the cognitive work she was supposed to in arriving at her belief on Sunday – and it seems she has. So, according to the deontological account of justification, it seems that she's justified in believing he will show up on Monday. (Don't forget: sometimes S is justified in believing p even though p is false. In those cases, of course, S doesn't know that p.)

This story shows why the deontological view of knowledge and justification is strongly connected with access internalism. It's reasonable to suppose that fulfilling your intellectual duty involves considering what's accessible to you. To decide whether to believe p or not, you consult the possible reasons for and against p – the ones you know about. How could you possibly consult the ones you don't know about?

Some questions about epistemic deontology

But it's not perfectly clear what fulfilling one's epistemic duties amounts to. Consider this modified version of the Alice and Zeke story:

> Alice remembers, on Sunday, that Zeke had told her to expect his arrival on Monday. Alice knows that Zeke is very reliable, so she believes he'll arrive then. But she's completely forgotten about Zeke's later phone call, telling her that he'd had to change his plans and would arrive on Tuesday instead.

On Sunday, based on what she knows then, Alice's mistaken belief is completely *internally* justified. She's gone over all the relevant facts she's aware of, and come to a completely reasonable belief, given those facts. What's missing is a crucial bit of evidence about Zeke's change of plans, but Alice doesn't remember this.

Should we count Alice as fulfilling her epistemic duties? It's tempting to say that fulfilling your duties means attending to all the relevant evidence you *have*, not to all the relevant evidence *there is*. If there's evidence S couldn't find out about, S is not to blame in not considering this. So the deontological view would say that her false belief is justified.

On the other hand, it's also tempting to say that Alice is not epistemically blameless here. She did attend to all the evidence she was aware of on Sunday, but she should have remembered Zeke's announcement of his change in plans. Maybe she could have remembered that on Sunday, if she had sat down and concentrated and asked herself if there's something she had forgotten. But even if she couldn't have remembered that on Sunday, earlier on she should have done things to make sure she did remember: she should have written down the information on her calendar, right after the phone call, for example.

The analogy with moral responsibility appears to reinforce this reply. Compare this story:

> Pete agrees to water Priscilla's houseplants while she's away, but he's forgotten where he put her keys and can't get into her apartment, and all the plants die.

Is Pete morally to blame? Once the keys are lost, he can't get into the house to water the plants. But, of course, he is to blame, because he should have taken care earlier to put her keys in a place where he could find them.

What this suggests is a bit of an expansion to epistemic deontology: to have satisfied your epistemic duties means not just consulting all your relevant beliefs, but also having acted, when appropriate, to make sure you're aware of additional, possibly relevant, facts. This can involve making sure earlier you don't forget what you knew then, or investigating later to make sure that there aren't relevant facts you're then unaware of.

Of course, it's not perfectly clear how much you're supposed to do. Alice and Zeke again:

> Alice remembers, on Sunday, that Zeke had told her to expect his arrival on Monday. Alice knows that Zeke is very reliable, so she believes he'll arrive then. But he's been in a car accident, and is in hospital unable to contact her to tell her he isn't coming.

Has Alice lived up to her epistemic responsibilities? There is *something* she could have done to find out the truth: she could have telephoned the hospital to find out if Zeke was there. But, of course, she had no reason to do this; it's not something that would reasonably be expected in a situation like this. Similarly, there's something that Pete could have done: he might have got a locksmith to let him into Priscilla's apartment, or he might have broken a window and climbed in, and then had the window repaired. But these are not things he would reasonably be expected to do, and be blamed for not doing.

The moral of all this is that it's a complicated matter to judge whether people have lived up to their responsibilities, ethical or epistemic, and there might be cases in which it's hard to decide. Nevertheless, the idea of responsibility is a valid one.

But here are some examples that can be taken to be more serious criticisms of epistemic deontology:

Adam is paranoid – he has a tendency to perceive threats where there aren't any. He thinks all the other people living in his apartment building are out to get him, plotting someday to steal his mail, to send the refrigerator repairman away when he comes to fix his fridge, and so on. So far nothing peculiar has happened in his building, and everyone acts friendly. When you point out these facts, he discounts them as insufficient to show anything. He just can't help feeling this way.

Betty is somewhat lacking in intelligence. The noises in her car, the bald tyres, the warning lights that keep flashing, and so on, point to imminent car trouble, but she just doesn't put two and two together, and remains blissfully sure that nothing will go wrong. (She's just very optimistic.) You can't even get her to understand things better when you try to explain.

Carl has been raised in a superstitious family, with contact only with other people who are similarly benighted. As a consequence, he shares all their unwarranted beliefs: that copper bracelets help with arthritis, that astrologers can predict your future, that sending money to TV evangelists will give you good luck. It's only natural that he believes all this – people he's talked to and lived around believe these things, and nobody has ever given him any reason to doubt them. His environment has provided him with no clue about reliable sources of information.

Dorothy knows plenty of good reasons to think that smoking is dangerous: she has heard health warnings from all sorts of sources that she admits are reliable, but all this, somehow, never really made an impression. 'Yeah, that's all true, but so what?' says Dorothy. But now her aunt, a heavy smoker, has died of emphysema. Impressed by this one case, she concludes solely on that basis that smoking really must be dangerous.

None of the four is blameworthy for their unsubstantiated beliefs – they're all doing their best to do their cognitive duty. You might want to say that there is nothing they should have done *and could have done* better to find things out. All four of them, it seems, have what epistemic deontologists might count as justified beliefs; but their beliefs are very clearly unjustified. In Dorothy's case, she even knows what really does justify her belief; it's just that she doesn't use that information as justification.

If you doubt that their beliefs are unjustified, try this thought-experiment. Imagine that some belief arising from Adam's paranoia, or Betty's ignorance, or Carl's superstition, turned out to be right, as Dorothy's does, just by accident. Wouldn't you agree that such a belief wasn't knowledge? It fails the justification condition.

Internalists, however, might reply that they wouldn't count these four as justified. Agreed that they're doing the best they can; but their best is not good enough. This reply, however, may be granting too much, relying as it does on a more objective 'external' view of what really counts as justification.

Next, consider these two cases:

Baby Ned always knows when Mum has come in the front door. After playing happily with the babysitter for hours, as soon as he hears Mum, he starts to scream.

Fido knows when it's time for dinner. Every afternoon at 5 pm he paces back and forth between his owner and his dog-dish, drooling a little.

Do you agree that both of these are cases of real knowledge? But they hardly appear to fit the epistemic deontologists' model.

In neither case do we imagine the believer examining his evidence, weighing it pro and con, and coming to a conclusion in conformity with his cognitive duties.

And last, consider this very ordinary example: you walk into the kitchen and see an apple somebody's put on the table. Your belief that there's an apple on the table arrives immediately when you see it. There's nothing here like weighing evidence, making sure that you haven't ignored or forgotten something, or anything else we've been thinking of as involved in your epistemic duty-fulfilment.

If it is to be plausible, then, the epistemic deontological position needs some further clarification or amendment. Philosophers have had a lot more to say in these directions than we can go into here. At this point, however, we should move on to consider externalist theories of knowledge.

The external connection

The cases of Baby Ned and Fido, and of the apple-in-the-kitchen, might be taken to show that the internalist picture of knowledge is mistaken, because in these cases, the duty-driven mental processes internalists describe are missing, but both Baby Ned and Fido have knowledge. And in the previous cases – paranoid Adam, dim Betty, superstitious Carl, and unreasoning Dorothy – performance of duty (to the best of their ability) seemed insufficient to make true belief knowledge, or false belief justified.

Well, if this is right, then let's ask: what is it about Baby Ned and Fido that means that their beliefs are knowledge? And what is missing in the cases of Adam, Betty, Carl, and Dorothy?

Externalists look beyond what is 'inside' the knower, to external conditions, for the necessary condition which, added to the others, makes the list sufficient for knowledge.

Consider, again, the analogy with ethics. Deontologists (internalists about ethics) consider only a person's motivation, holding that if the action is motivated by the desire to do one's duty, it's a good action. But externalists about ethics argue that what should be considered instead, when evaluating the action, is its actual effects in the world. A duty-motivated action can in fact have very bad unintended results. Similarly, the epistemic externalist argues that trying one's best to justify one's belief isn't what's relevant for knowledge.

What, then, must be true 'externally' when S knows that p, according to the externalist? Clearly it's not merely the *actual truth* of p. Everyone – internalists and externalists – agree that this is necessary but not sufficient. As we've seen, there's a strong tradition of adding that the *belief that* p must be justified, and many externalists concentrate on this condition, giving an external account of justification.

Clearly again, however, no externalist wants to give a wholly external account of justification – that is, that there merely exist sufficient justification for p, whatever the cognitive state of S. Consider these examples:

> Smedley has committed a murder, and he has buried the knife he used, covered with his fingerprints and the victim's blood, in his backyard. This knife is conclusive evidence that Smedley did it, but nobody has thought to dig around in the backyard and it remains buried. Police Sergeant Thursday has a strong hunch, but no evidence, that Smedley is the murderer. He says, 'I just know Smedley did it.' When the evidence eventually turns up, Thursday says, 'I knew it.'

Did Thursday *know* (before the evidence turned up) that Smedley did it? He believed it, and it was true. What he meant when he said he knew it was probably just that he felt certain. The only evidence he *had* at the time wasn't enough to entitle him to make the claim he did. Justification for his claim existed

– the bloodstained fingerprinted knife – but nobody found that till much later. We're inclined, I think, to say that he didn't know that Smedley did it. His belief (however strongly held) was a good guess, based on insufficient evidence.

What this appears to show is that the *existence* of justifying evidence is not sufficient to grant S knowledge. Externalists would agree. They would require, in addition, that the evidence (in some sense) be available to S.

You might recall the example of Noreen, who can predict who'll win the World Cup. A much more recent version of this sort of story, one that's referred to often by philosophers, is this:

> Norman the Clairvoyant mysteriously believes that the President is in New York exactly when he is, though Norman has no idea how he came to believe this, and it's clear that none of the usual mechanisms is operating: that is, nobody told him, he didn't see the motorcade on TV, he didn't read about the President's visit in the newspaper, and so on.

Externalism would judge that Norman has knowledge. But, it's argued, he doesn't. Norman's beliefs are unjustified – irrational – because those beliefs just pop into his head, without supporting reasons (as Norman himself will be the first to confirm). But whatever his method is, his beliefs are reliably true, so apparently justified.

Of course, the suggestion that Norman's method – clairvoyance – gives him reliable information would be met with scepticism by all intelligent people. Clairvoyance is classed with astrology, extrasensory perception, fortune-telling, palm-reading, dream interpretation, previous-life regression, near-death experiences, telepathy, and holistic medicine as either totally unreliable or completely fraudulent belief-production mechanisms. But Norman's clairvoyance (according to the story) really is reliable, though currently unrecognized by science. So, externalists would reply, although it's a conclusion reasonable people would initially resist, Norman in fact does have justified belief, and this is knowledge.

If Barbie, in the example we considered earlier, never becomes aware of the basis for her belief, externalists would nevertheless credit her with knowledge that it's been snowing. There was adequate evidence for that belief, and she *had* that evidence; it was the source of her belief. But what does it mean to say that the evidence was the source of her belief?

Imagine that Adam really is being plotted against, so his paranoid belief is true, but not knowledge. The reason, apparently, is that he came to this belief in the wrong sort of way, via his paranoia. Similarly, Carl's superstitions disconnect his beliefs from the real facts of the world, as do Betty's cognitive difficulties. Baby Ned's belief that Mum is home, by contrast, arises when she actually arrives, as a result of that arrival; that's why he gets it right. Similarly, Fido, we expect, has some sort of hunger and timing mechanism in him that produces the appropriate response connected to the time of day.

What an account of genuine knowledge needs to insist on, it seems, is the right sort of connection with the external world; this is what would make the truth of a belief not merely a matter of accident. It's this approach which is taken by the causal theory, which we'll examine now.

The causal theory

In the background of much of what we have been assuming so far is the idea that S must have reasons for the belief that p; but the causal theory represents a radical departure from this traditional assumption. We have been operating on the assumption that a justification for a belief consists in the reasons S has for that belief – that is, in S's evidence. But the **causal theory** looks at the *causes* of S's belief, rather than the reasons or evidence S has.

It argues that to count as knowledge, S's true belief that p must be causally connected to the fact that p. This makes the causal theory an externalist theory, concentrating on the facts external to S.

Instead of saying that S's belief that p is justified if it is supported by appropriate evidence that S has for p, the causal theory urges us to consider whether S's belief is caused by the fact that p, in the right sort of way. A controversial view of some philosophers is that reasons are a type of cause – that is, that we should understand the reasons S has as causes for what S does. But there are other sorts of causes for what one does as well. On this view, then, the causal theory would accept as knowledge true belief that p accompanied by the right sort of reasons (causes of the belief traceable back to p), but would add that other sorts of cause would make for knowledge as well.

The causal theory appealed to many philosophers because it gave results that matched our intuitions about many cases. Fido and Baby Ned's beliefs are caused by the facts they believe in, and that's why we count them as knowing these facts, even though they lack a full-fledged apparatus for rational deliberation. If we suppose Adam's paranoid belief to be, in fact, true, the causal theory correctly would count this as not a case of knowledge, because the fact that he is being plotted against doesn't cause his belief: it's caused by his paranoia. Some Gettier difficulties can be dealt with as well. Recall the case of Max and the decoy ducks. The fact that there were real ducks on the lake wasn't causally connected with his (true) belief that there were. It was caused by the presence of the decoy ducks. That explains, according to the causal theory, why he didn't have knowledge.

In cases such as these, the causal theory explains our intuition that the beliefs in question weren't justified. But it does not give us an account of justification. Recall the important fact that there can be justification for p when p is false; but in that sort of case, of course, the belief that p is not causally connected with the fact that p – there is no such fact. The causal connection required by the causal theory can occur only in cases in which the belief is true. Thus the causal theory offers us not an account of what justification is, but rather a substitute for the justification condition.

Problems with the causal theory

Here's a criticism of the causal theory. Usually philosophers say that only *events* are causes – things that happen at a particular time. Now, surely we know truths of arithmetic, but the facts that make them true aren't events – they're eternal – so they can't be causes. Well, causal theorists are aware of this, and make an exception for this case; but this does put some strain on the theory. (Providing an account of the source of our knowledge of arithmetic, and of the kind of facts arithmetical truths report, has always provided a challenge for philosophers.)

Here's another problem, perhaps dealt with quite easily. Consider this modified version of the Alice/Zeke story, with no complication about inference and no Gettier problem:

> Zeke tells Alice on Friday morning that he'll arrive in town on Saturday. He's very responsible and reliable, and on Friday Alice believes what he says. He arrives, as he said he would, on Saturday.

This is a straightforward example of knowledge, but it appears to present a problem for the causal theory, because in this case the fact that he arrives on Saturday clearly couldn't cause Alice's belief on Friday. That's because causes never come after their effects.

But those who advocate the causal theory are aware of this sort of potential problem, and they're careful to avoid it. They don't say that a necessary condition for *S knows that p* is that *the fact that p* causes *S's belief that p*. They say that a necessary condition is that the fact that p is *causally connected* with S's belief that p. In the latest Zeke/Alice story, Zeke's arrival on Saturday and Alice's belief on Friday have a joint cause: Zeke's reliable intention back on Friday.

Now recall the original Joan/Jack/Jim Gettier-type example. Joan believes that there is that dreaded letter in her mailbox, and her reason is the false belief that Jack got the job, itself caused by what the office gossip told her. But none of this is causally connected to the fact that there's that letter in her mailbox. The events causally connected with that letter's being there – its causes – have to do with Jim's getting the job, not with Jack. So there's no causal connection between her belief and the fact that she believes. It's just a coincidence, and it's not knowledge. So far so good for the causal theory.

But, sadly, there are still problems here. Let's add some details to the Joan/Jack/Jim story, as follows. Suppose that the reason the office gossip thought that Jack was going to get the job was that he saw a note on the big boss's desk saying 'TELL HEAD OFFICE THAT J. HAS THE JOB'. The reason the note was there was that *Jim* had been given the job; the office gossip didn't even know that Jim was in the running, and just assumed it was Jack. That's why he told Joan that Jack got the job. Now, when we trace back the causal antecedents of Joan's belief that the letter was in her mailbox, we go back to her belief that Jack got the job, back from there to the gossip's belief that Jack got it, back from there to the note, and back from there to the fact that *Jim* got the job. And tracing forward in another causal chain from the fact that Jim got the job, we come to the presence of the letter. So, after all, the presence of the letter and Joan's belief that the letter is there *do* have a causal connection. But it's still clear, after having made all these elaborate additions to the story, that Joan does not know that letter is there.

Again, the proposers of the causal theory are aware of this sort of response. What they say, in defence of their position, is that not just any causal connection will do to establish knowledge. Some causal connections are not of the right sort to certify S's belief as knowledge. So, they say, to save the causal theory, we need an account of what's the *right sort* of causal connection; and they're working on this. But this complication makes many critics reject the causal theory because of what they think is the hopeless problem of specifying what makes a causal connection count as the right sort.

The following story raises still a further problem for the causal theory:

> Horace knows a barn when he sees one. He's now driving through an area where, unbeknown to him, they're making a movie, and they've erected a whole lot of fake barns – they're just facades, but they really look like barns from the front, seen from the road. Horace sees what is in fact the one real barn in the area, and this results in his belief that there's a barn.

This story satisfies the conditions for knowledge given by the causal theory: the fact that there is a barn there causes (very directly, in this case) Horace's true belief. But the usual reaction to this story is that Horace doesn't know that there's a barn there. It may be possible to fix the causal theory to take care of this counter-example and others like it; but some philosophers think that these show that causal theory just won't work, and some of them look to other externalist theories.

Reliabilism

This is an externalist theory that attempts to avoid some of the problems facing the causal theory, most notably the problem of specifying what in general the right sort of causal connection would be.

Reliabilism is usually taken to be a theory of justification (unlike the causal theory); if it can avoid Gettier and other problems by its notion of justification, then the traditional account of knowledge as justified true belief can be revived.

The idea behind reliabilism is simple: a belief is justified when it arises from (or is sustained by) a reliable belief-formation mechanism. A reliable mechanism is one that tends to produce true beliefs. The intention here is to rule out Gettier-type cases in which true belief isn't knowledge, because it arises just by accident; it's supposed, then, that a better understanding of justification would show that belief really isn't justified in those cases.

A theory closely related to reliabilism, one you may see reference to in your readings, is called the **truth-tracking theory**. This says, basically, that there's knowledge when S's cognitive system 'tracks the truth' analogously to the way that the indications on a thermometer track the temperature. So if it's raining, you believe it's raining, and if it isn't you don't believe it is. This theory differs from reliabilism in some technical ways, but much of what we'll say about reliabilism applies to truth-tracking as well.

The important feature of reliabilism, the one that distinguishes it from some other theories, is that whether or not a particular belief of S's is knowledge depends on the *method* actually used by S to get that belief, and on the *history of the use* of that method: for that belief to count as knowledge, that method has to have a history of success in producing true beliefs – not always, but very often. (Just how often is something that isn't specified, and probably can't be.)

However, let's see how reliabilism fares on some examples that produce problems elsewhere.

What should we say about Joan and her office problem? The problem in this case arose because we were tempted to say that

Joan's belief was justified – it came from testimony from the usually very reliable office gossip. Reliabilism thus runs into exactly the same Gettier-type difficulty. The reliabilist might want to reply that, given the *full* story as imagined, the method turned out to be unreliable: trusting an informant who jumps to conclusions is not a reliable method. Note, however, that whenever there is a false but apparently justified conclusion, one might specify the method with enough detail so as to demonstrate its unreliability. The following example provides an illustration of the relativity of reliability to different specifications of method:

> Cora is very good at recognizing faces. She identifies someone as Benjy by seeing him from a distance, but it's actually Benjy's long lost identical twin.

Is Cora's method reliable or not? Well, that depends on how we specify the method. If we consider her method as *the use of facial features to identify people,* her method is very reliable. But if we consider her method as *the use of facial features to identify one of two identical twins,* then her method is quite unreliable. Reliabilism needs to provide, then, a principle for specifying which method we're considering. This may pose comparable difficulties to the ones faced by the causal theory, of specifying what causal links are the right ones. It could be that the apparent comparative advantage of reliabilism has disappeared.

Let's now go back to Barn Country, and see what reliabilism has to say about Horace. Recall that usually he's a reliable identifier of barns, and when (unknown to him) he's in an area in which what look like barns are almost entirely fake barn-facades, he happens by chance to see a real barn and identify it correctly. But he doesn't know there's a barn there. Causal theory gave the wrong answer, because Horace's belief that a barn is in front of him is caused in a very direct and ordinary way by the fact that there is a barn in front of him. But reliabilism might do better. We've assumed that Horace is a reliable barn-detector (he's done it consistently correctly lots of times); but the problem in this example is that, in Barn Country, he's not a reliable barn-detector. Even though he hasn't seen any of the facades, they're designed to look just like real barns, and he'd be fooled into thinking they were. His success in this case is just lucky, and rather improbable, given the rarity of real barns among the plentiful facades in Barn Country. Relative to his current location in Barn Country, then, his method of barn-detection is not reliable. That's why, a reliabilist would say, he's not justified in his true belief, and he doesn't know there's a barn there.

We should note two features of the way reliabilism would treat this example. First, recall that we introduced the idea of *a reliable method* by saying that it's one that's worked well in the past (implying, of course, that an unreliable method is one that didn't). Horace's method of barn-detection in Barn Country, it's clear, is unreliable, but not because it hasn't worked well in the past. He's never tried to identify a barn in Barn Country before, nor has he ever seen and misidentified a barn-facade. His method is unreliable because *if* he had seen a barn-facade, he *would have* misidentified it as a barn. So to pursue reliabilism, we'd have to fix our account of reliability/unreliability along these lines. This seems doable. But second, note that his method is unreliable in Barn Country but reliable everywhere else (because there are almost no barn-facades elsewhere). So we need to relativize reliability/unreliability to the believer's context. Again, we need principles directing us how to do this. Note that we get different answers if we choose different contexts. Suppose that Horace is in the middle of the Old MacDonald Farm, a few acres of Barn Country in which no facades have been erected, so that the MacDonald (real) barn is the only one in sight. Relative to this smaller context, Horace's barn-detection is reliable. Which context is the relevant one?

> The position that the truth or falsity of knowledge claims is relative to context is called **contextualism**.

Finally, two similar sorts of problem. Reliabilism wants to judge each individual belief on the basis of considerations about the process of belief-formation that accounted for it in general. But to apply this, we have to specify which of many possible belief-formation processes to look at. Consider the example of my belief about where I left my keys this morning, based on my memory. This is an example of memory; but it's also an example of more particular kinds of memory, for example, memories of:

events earlier in the day
events earlier in the week
routine habitual actions of mine
things I did earlier in the day
where I left something
where I put my keys
something that happened during the past year
something that happened in my house

and on and on. So this particular process can be considered as one of an infinite number of different *kinds* of process. Which one is the kind of process we're supposed to evaluate for reliability, or for truth-tracking? It makes a difference which one we pick. I might be quite reliable at remembering something that I did earlier in the day, but not very good at all at remembering routine habitual actions (which I do mindlessly, and usually forget or misremember). So we can't decide whether the kind of process responsible for this particular belief is reliable till we've decided what kind of process it is. It's not at all clear how, in general, we should do this. What's the relevant process-type here? This is something else that needs to be specified.

Next, consider Horace in the context of Barn Country. He's not a reliable barn-detector there, so (reliabilism judges) relative to this context, his belief that there's a barn in front of him is not knowledge. Now, suppose in addition, that the barn he sees is red, but all the barn facades in Barn Country are other colours. In this same context, then, he's a very good *red* barn-detector, and his belief that there's a *red* barn there is knowledge. So we'd have to say that relative to Barn Country, Horace knows that there's a red barn there, but he doesn't know that there's a barn there. But the proposition *There's a red barn there* entails the proposition *There's a barn there*, and we can suppose that Horace knows this elementary fact of logic. So Horace knows that p, and he knows that p entails q, but he doesn't know that q. This is an odd Gettier-like consequence of reliabilism. Is it a problem, or should we just accept the peculiarity?

We have concluded our considerations of various externalist and internalist theories, without having settled on any one of them. This represents the current philosophical state of play: all the varieties of theory have their partisans, who are working to try to get around the objections we've looked at – and more.

5
Foundationalism and coherentism

Foundationalism – the regress argument

A major division between epistemologists for centuries has concerned the structure of what we know. Clearly, some of our beliefs depend on other beliefs for their justification. **Foundationalism** is (roughly speaking) the position that some beliefs, however, are 'foundations' for all the rest – that is, they justify other beliefs, but are themselves not justified. **Coherentism** is the competing view: it recognizes no foundational beliefs, but sees each belief as justifying, and being justified by, other beliefs. In this chapter, we'll explore and elaborate on each of these two positions, looking at and evaluating the arguments for and against each.

A very old argument in favour of foundationalism, dating back at least to Aristotle's mid-fourth-century BCE version of it, is the **epistemic regress argument**. Here it is.

Let's assume that justification of one belief involves support by a different belief – actually, typically, several different beliefs. So, for example, if I ask you for justification for your belief that it's going to snow tomorrow, you report a couple of other things you believe: that it was predicted on the radio this morning, and that short-term weather predictions like this on the radio are pretty reliable. What's going on here can be seen as a species of **logical inference**: from these two beliefs, you infer the one in question. This need not be **deductive inference** – entailment – in which what's inferred follows necessarily from the premises (for example: *Every dog barks; Fido is a dog; therefore Fido barks*). It can also be **inductive inference**, in which the premises give some plausibility to the conclusion (*Logic tests are usually held on a Friday, so we can conclude that next week's test will also be on a Friday*).

Note that in order for this inference to produce justification, the premises of your inference – the beliefs you infer *from* – must themselves be acceptable. They might themselves be justified by inference from still further beliefs. So does *every* acceptable belief have to be supported in this way? If so, then if belief B supports belief A, then we'd need a belief C to support B, and a belief D to support C, and so on. This produces a **justificatory chain**.

Now consider the possible structures of these chains. (For simplicity, I'll just talk as if each belief is supported by one other belief, but you should understand that often inferential support comes from more than one other.)

Structure 1 Such a chain might be endless, with every 'link' in it receiving support from another belief, forever, infinitely.

Structure 2 Or else, such a chain might go in a circle, for example with A supported by B, B supported by C, C supported by D, and D supported by A.

Structure 3 Or else such a chain is finite, for example, with A supported by B, B supported by C, C supported by D, and that's the end of it: D isn't supported by anything else.

Let's have a closer look at these three possible structures.

Structure 1 has problems. For justification of any of S's beliefs, S would need an infinite number of other beliefs. Is this possible?

Intuitively, it seems that we only have a finite capacity for belief, and once this is reached, something has to be dropped for something else to be added. (My finite memory seems to work this way: for me to remember something new, I have to forget something else.) Is this correct?

Here's an example of what maybe would count as an infinite number of beliefs that you have right now. You believe that there is no largest positive integer, right? (Positive integers, in case you've forgotten your arithmetic, are the numbers 0, 1, 2, 3, etc.) So you believe:

0 is not the largest positive integer, because there's a larger one, namely 1.

1 is not the largest positive integer, because there's a larger one, namely 2.

2 is not the largest positive integer, because ...

Should I go on? No, you get the idea. So there are an infinite number of beliefs here, right?

Well, some philosophers would object that there's really not an infinite number of beliefs here. What there is, is a *potentially* infinite number. That means that, given any integer x, no matter what, you'll believe there's a next-higher one, x + 1. So the number of *possible* beliefs you have the potential to have is infinite, but the number of *actual* beliefs you have is finite. Here's an analogy. Suppose you started writing down the sequence of positive integers, 0, 1, 2, 3, and so on. Wherever you were in this series, you could write down the next one – *potentially* an infinite number of numbers. But the number of numbers you would have *actually* written down would always be finite.

You may recall from our earlier discussion of Ayer's position on justification, the proposal that one needn't be actively thinking that p in order to believe p: it's enough for you to have the potential to affirm that p if you did consider that proposition. So if beliefs need only be potential thoughts, you could have an infinite number of these.

On the other hand, consider this:

A is justified if B is.
B is justified if C is.
C is justified if D is.
D is justified if ...

and so on. But in each case we only have **hypothetical justification** – *justification if*. This doesn't turn into justification unless, somewhere along the line, there is something that's not merely hypothetically justified, but is *just plain justified* – something that we should call **categorically justified**. Consider this analogy: suppose

Alice wants to go to the party if Ben wants to.
Ben wants to go to the party if Carol wants to.
Carol wants to go to the party if Donald wants to.
Donald wants ...

and so on. If everyone just hypothetically wants to go to the party – nobody categorically wants to go, just wants to go, no ifs about it – then this doesn't result in anyone's wanting to go. Similarly, even an infinite number of these hypothetical justifications doesn't add up to anything actually being justified.

These arguments cast grave doubt on the Structure 1 proposal.

There are some serious objections to be raised to Structure 2 also. It seems, for one thing, that we again face the problem that this would only provide hypothetical support for everything in the circle. A is justified if B is; B is justified if C is; C is justified if D is; and D is justified if A is. Again nothing provides categorical justification. By analogy, imagine four friends are wondering about whether to go to the party.

Alice wants to go if Ben wants to.
Ben wants to go if Carol wants to.
Carol wants to go if Donald wants to.
Donald wants to go if Alice wants to.

No progress has been made in deciding whether anyone wants to go.

It appears that Structure 2 is just as implausible as Structure 1. Rejecting this, we are left with Structure 3, the only remaining possibility.

Acceptable but unsupported beliefs

If Structure 3 is the only possible justificatory structure for our beliefs, then there must be some beliefs that support other beliefs but are themselves unsupported. We'll call these **basic beliefs**.

Basic beliefs are unsupported by other beliefs, but does that make them all just guesses or hunches – illicit or irrational? If some basic beliefs are acceptable, why those?

Some foundationalists have wanted to answer this question by saying that basic beliefs are acceptable when they're *self*-justifying. But you can see why many philosophers find this an unsatisfactory account. It sounds like what's being claimed is that some beliefs hold themselves up by their own bootstraps. Compare:

> FRED: It's going to snow tomorrow.
> NED: Really? What reason do you have to think that?
> FRED: Because it's going to snow tomorrow.

Fred's reply, of course, provides no support for his earlier assertion.

Descartes was a foundationalist. As we've seen, he required infallibility for beliefs that counted as genuine knowledge; these (supposedly) infallible beliefs acted for him as basic beliefs. We can see the connection between infallibility and foundational status. If a belief was fallible, then it might be wrong. If it might be wrong, one would need some assurance that it's correct. Otherwise, there would be no difference between an acceptable belief and an unacceptable guess. But there won't be other acceptable beliefs providing evidence in its favour if the belief is basic. So the only way a basic belief can be acceptable, it seems, is if it's infallible.

The most famous allegedly basic and infallible belief Descartes talks about is his belief that he exists. It's infallible because he can't be mistaken about it. No matter what other mistakes he makes, he can't be mistaken about this one, because any sort of thinking, correct or mistaken, can only be done by an existing thinking being. He also supposes the existence of God to be demonstrable with certainty, infallibly; and next a variety of beliefs in the areas of mathematics and geometry – beliefs guaranteed infallible by God provided we follow the proper methodology in deriving them. Moreover, he claims infallibility of beliefs about the content of our own minds.

> Remember *cogito ergo sum*? Everyone's heard of this. By this slogan ('I think, therefore I am') Descartes sums up his argument that this belief is infallible.

But it's questionable whether there are any infallible beliefs. Ayer, as we've seen, objected to infallibility on the grounds that there's no logical impossibility in supposing that S believes p but p is false. (He was, however, inclined to grant that belief in one's own existence, which does seem to involve this kind of impossibility, was infallible.) We'll have a closer look at some of these sorts of knowledge later in this book, in the section on rationalism. But for the moment, you should note that even if Descartes is right about the infallibility of the beliefs in his own existence and God's, and in the propositions of mathematics and geometry, it doesn't seem that these can get us very far as foundations for other sorts of knowledge. Just try to derive your knowledge that elephants are bigger than fleas from these foundations.

Descartes was unwilling to grant any beliefs that arose from perception as knowledge, but a long-standing tradition has arisen among foundationalists to give certain basic perceptual statements the infallibility they thought the foundation of knowledge should have. The problem is (some philosophers have thought) that ordinary **empirical** beliefs – beliefs arising from perception, for example, S's belief that there's an apple there – are hardly good candidates for infallibility. Illusions, hallucinations, and dreaming can lead to false beliefs, and it's possible that any of this sort of belief could be wrong. Anyway, it seems, S's belief that there's an apple out there is not basic: it's justified by S's belief that he or she's having apple-like visual experiences. That belief, about one's sense-experience, may be basic, and it may be infallible too. Whether or not there's really an apple in front of S, S can't be wrong about that visual experience, so (some philosophers have argued) we have infallible beliefs about our own experience. If this is correct, however, we still have that problem about elephants and fleas.

Modest foundationalism

But maybe basic beliefs don't need to be infallible. Many contemporary foundationalists favour **modest foundationalism**, the view that basic beliefs may be fallible. This seems to be a good deal more true-to-life. It's pretty obvious (though, of course, philosophically disputable) that we do have fallible beliefs of various sorts – those arising from perception, for example – and that some of these beliefs are basic. The question modest foundationalism must face is that, if the alleged foundations are not infallible, why are they acceptable?

One answer to this question which has found favour with many contemporary modest foundationalists is that our basic empirical beliefs, while not supported by inference from other beliefs, are not therefore unsupported. Modest foundationalists take many perceptual beliefs to be well supported, by our perceptual experience. Earlier we didn't define basic beliefs as beliefs without *any* support – just without support from any other beliefs. Why suppose that inference from other beliefs is the only sort of support a belief might have?

Here's what may be an answer to that question, and a criticism of this sort of foundationalism. We know what it is for one belief (or several) to support another. The belief that p supports the belief that q when p logically entails q, or when p provides good inductive evidence for q. But we have no good account of what it is for a belief to be supported by something that is not itself a belief. But how can an experience be support for a belief? Is there supposed to be some connection between an experience and the proposition which is the object of the belief it supports?

Coherentism

Coherentists deny that Structure 2 is to be rejected; that structure, in a sense, describes their picture of justification. Only in a sense, however. Possibility 2 still envisions justification chains as linear (with the end of the chain linking to the beginning), whereas coherentists use different metaphors, most notably a 'web of belief'. What this means is that each belief is connected to several others, and our body of beliefs altogether is formed by this interlocking collection. According to this picture, there are no basic beliefs: each belief in this web is supported by one or more others. We do have something like circularity here, in that if you trace along this web long enough you will come back to where you started from, but it's by no means a simple circle. Coherentists sometimes speak of justification, then, as 'holistic', as opposed to 'linear' (or to 'circular', for that matter).

The originator of the 'web of belief' metaphor for a coherentist view is the American philosopher Willard Van Orman Quine (1908–2000), considered by some to be the foremost English-speaking philosopher of the twentieth century.

Coherentists disagree with the foundationalists who claim that some beliefs are basic: self-justifying, or infallible, or justified by experience, independently of other beliefs. Every belief in this web of belief is supported by other beliefs; but that means that every belief is subject to withdrawal, if its support were withdrawn, or other beliefs turn up which are contrary to it. This would do away with the idea that some of our beliefs that arise from perception are rock-solid and unchangeable no matter what, as well as with the sorts of belief that Descartes thought infallible, indubitable, and incorrigible. Everything would be up for grabs.

One feature of this holistic structure is that justification does not go just in one direction. We have been supposing, so far, that the items in this structure are beliefs, and that the justification-relation is that of logical inference – entailment from premises to conclusion. But coherentists emphasize that the support beliefs give to each other can go in both directions: if S's belief that p justifies S's belief that q, then to some extent, it will work the other way too, with S's belief that q justifying S's belief that p. For example, suppose that Brenda believes the test will happen next Friday because they usually happen on Friday. In this situation, her belief that they usually happen on Friday justifies her belief that it will happen this Friday. But things can work the other way around: when it turns out that the test is, in fact, on Friday, this acts as further justification for her more general belief that tests usually happen on Friday. Neither belief is more basic; each reinforces the other. Similarly, the opposite of justification ('falsification') can work in either direction too. Suppose you believe that all swans are white, and you think you see a black swan. You might decide that you were wrong, after all, in your belief that all swans are white; but you might decide, instead, that what you saw wasn't really a black swan – maybe it was some other sort of bird, or maybe there was some sort of trick of the light that just made it look black.

But thinking of the relation between these beliefs as logical inference is perhaps too narrow. Contemporary coherentists often add that the relation can be explanatory – one belief (or set of beliefs) produces explanation for another, in the way a scientific theory can provide explanation for particular data.

A **scientific theory** has a much more complicated structure than a simple logical entailment from premises to conclusion, or an inference supporting a general statement by producing specific instances in which it's true. A theory is made up of a number of generalizations, some of them typically referring to unobserved things postulated because they make for the best overall theory, plus a number of observation-statements, typically from a variety of different contexts, which confirm the theory – which are consistent with it, and which are best explained by the theory. Inference involving particular observations can work in two ways: it can help confirm (or disconfirm) the theory; but the theory can in turn reinforce or cast doubt on the validity of the particular observations.

You should be careful to note that when scientists and philosophers of science speak of a 'theory', they don't mean what that term sometimes means in ordinary talk: just a guess or a so-far insufficiently confirmed hypothesis. (Think of the atomic theory, or of the continental-drift theory in geology.)

Although many coherentists take the web they're talking about to be a web of *beliefs* – containing interlocking beliefs only – some want to add *experiences* (as opposed to beliefs about experiences) to the web of justification. They face, however, the same problem as foundationalists do with this move: the necessity of explaining how an experience can justify a belief. But there's a special problem here for coherentists, who emphasize two-way justification, as we've seen. They'd need to explain what is quite puzzling: what it means for a belief to justify an experience. To justify something in this context means to make it more believable, or more likely to be true; but experiences (unlike beliefs) are not things one believes, and, not having propositional content, are neither true nor false. But if coherentists take it that the experiences in the web have the function of justifying beliefs, but are not themselves capable of justification, then we're back with foundationalism.

Coherentism has some clear advantages. It avoids what many philosophers consider implausible – the idea of a basic belief. Against this idea, they sometimes argue that it always makes sense, for every one of everyone's beliefs, to ask, 'What's your justification for believing that?' Coherentism provides a model in which (in theory) there's always an answer to that; but at the same time it does not rely on the equally implausible idea that there can be an infinite number of beliefs.

A second advantage is that, as we've seen, it appears unlikely that a proposed foundation – Descartes' supposedly infallible beliefs, for example, or the empiricists' beliefs about present sense experiences – can support the structure of our knowledge. Belief in one's own existence doesn't seem to imply much about the real world, and neither does any belief about our perceptual experience, just by itself. Consider the beliefs you count as knowledge about the past and the future, about unobserved theoretical entities in science, about other people's mental states, about ethics, and so on. How could these be derived from any simple foundation?

Criticisms of coherentism

First, notice this feature of coherentism: when any candidate for a new belief comes along, you see whether it coheres with all the rest of your beliefs to judge its acceptability. This is presumably true even for all the myriad of trivial beliefs that crop up every minute: *the sun is shining, the sun is still shining, I'm hungry, there's a dog, the dog has passed* ... But this check-up would certainly be very difficult, perhaps even impossible, given the number of your beliefs. Add to this the problem that maybe at times you don't even know whether you believe a particular proposition or not. For example: do you have a belief about what day of the week Christmas came on last year? I don't know whether I have any beliefs about this or not. If I think about it for a long while I may be able to dredge up something.

Coherentists might reply to this criticism that it's not just a problem for their theory. Any theory of how we judge new information would have to have a place for checking whether it's consistent with what we already believe. No doubt explaining exactly how this works is a tricky matter, probably needing some information from psychologists who have investigated it. But anyway, it seems clear that new belief-candidates don't have to be checked against everything we believe, just against relevant beliefs – and not even all of them. Everyone has had the experience of discovering a lack of coherence in their web of beliefs long after the new one that's caused the problem has been added. So it's clearly a perfectly excusable part of normal rational belief-acquisition procedure not to check for problems *everywhere* in our web.

Here is a second problem. Imagine that you believe on Sunday that Erica will arrive on Tuesday. This belief is strongly integrated into a number of other beliefs: that Erica almost always arrives on Tuesdays, that she, Kaia, Anna, and George all told you that she's coming this Tuesday, and so on. According to the coherentist, this belief is strongly justified (and this seems right). But suppose that on Monday you open the front door and *see* Erica right there in front of you. Now you no longer believe that Erica won't come till Tuesday, nor should you. But the belief that Erica won't arrive till Tuesday is the one that coheres very strongly in your web of belief, so it's the one, according to coherentists, that would be more strongly justified. But this is obviously wrong. The right response to this example appears to be that seeing Erica is conclusive. It seems that the belief resulting from experience is a basic belief, a foundation.

Several strategies for reply to this criticism are available for the coherentist. (1) The coherentist isn't committed to the view that an experience can't overrule a number of reasons to think otherwise. Think about all those beliefs that cohere with trusting your senses: you believe your eyes are trustworthy (under good conditions for observation); you believe you can recognize Erica; and so on. So maybe, after all, it's more strongly coherent with your web of beliefs to trust your perception. (2) Quine in fact, allows that the web of belief can give a sort of priority – extra strength – to experience. The problem here is that this may be giving too much away to the foundationalists. (3) But sometimes a lot of other reasons to believe something *can and should* overrule this sort of immediate experience-belief in something else. You reject beliefs based on immediate experience as illusions or hallucinations or simple mistakes when this happens. In general, the coherentist view is rather conservative, in that it emphasizes that new candidates for belief are overruled when they conflict with too much existing belief. But that's the way it *should* be, isn't it?

But coherentists face a more difficult challenge to their claim that every belief can be refused admittance or overturned when it comes to those beliefs that Descartes considered infallible. How could there be anything in our web of beliefs that could possibly lead us to deny that $1 + 2 = 3$? The same problem applies to logical truths, such as *The test is on Tuesday or it isn't.*

But here's what is usually taken to be the main difficulty with coherentism. Consider this example, the **Flat-Earth Theory**:

The Earth is a flat disc; it has a diameter of about 25,000 miles, and has the North Pole at its centre and a high wall of ice all around the edges. The Sun and the Moon are both discs, each about thirty-six miles in diameter, revolving above the disc, thus causing night and day. The Earth's disc is accelerating upward, causing gravity. If the Earth were a sphere, Flat-Earthers argue, large bodies of water would have a curved surface, but careful measurements of large lakes have shown none. Photographs of the Earth taken by astronauts appearing to show a sphere are either optical illusions or fakes produced by a NASA conspiracy with the news media, and so are those TV transmissions supposed to be from the Moon. The phases of the Moon are explained by the assumption that an invisible dark disc passes gradually in front of it. And so on.

Notice what's going on here. An interlocking set of beliefs is created, many of which are inconsistent with common sense or with conventionally accepted science. Observations that seem to conflict with this theory are explained away by ad hoc adjustments to the theory, or by rejecting them as lies from a conspiracy to deceive. The aim here, pursued with a considerable amount of imagination, effort, and intelligence, is a coherent system of beliefs. It may be coherent, but it's almost entirely false.

So that's the main problem with the coherentist account of justification. It seems that any proposition – true or false – might be surrounded by others interlocking with it in the appropriately explanatory way – just as long as we don't care if anything in the whole works is true or not. Internal coherence is an important criterion for the fictional world pictured in a good novel – but of course, that world may have not much to do with reality. So a web of beliefs that's perfectly satisfactory, according to coherence standards, might contain a preponderance of false statements.

Coherence is, of course, a virtue for systems of belief: we wouldn't want our beliefs to be radically inconsistent, or with large isolated areas, unconnected by explanatory or inferential links with the rest. But any number of mutually incompatible but internally coherent belief-webs can be cooked up; more than one of these coherent webs can't be true, but coherence theory doesn't say anything about this. This shows, according to critics of coherentism, that while coherence may be necessary for justification, it can't be sufficient. Justification has to have something to do with connecting beliefs to the outside world, but coherence pays no attention to this matter. (So it is, in a way, an internalist view.)

To these objections, there are several sorts of reply by coherentists. First, consider two internally coherent but mutually contradictory belief systems. According to the coherentist, there would be no rational way to choose between them. But is this

Here's an example of the conflict of two such systems. A half-century ago, the dominant geological theory explaining mountains, earthquakes, and so on involved the idea that the surface of the Earth was cooling, and thus shrinking (like the skin of a drying-out orange) and consequently cracking and wrinkling. A competing theory postulated that the Earth's surface was made of continent-sized plates, drifting around floating on a molten core; these plates bumped into each other, pushing each other up or down, sticking against each other and separating. This theory, proposed in something like its modern form in 1915, was considered crackpot for years; but towards the middle of the twentieth century became a serious competitor for the existing view. At that point the two incompatible theories each had a good deal of internal coherence; each relied on its own favourite evidence, explaining away other apparently contrary observations. For a while, scientists were divided about which to accept. But soon the continental-drift theory, which had added more evidence and more explanatory mechanism, replaced the old one. The point, for our purposes, is that the idea that competing, incompatible but internally coherent webs can – and do – coexist, at least for a while.

really a problem for coherentism? If there were two such systems (and the history of ideas provides several real-life examples) then isn't the coherentist response — that given equal internal coherence, there's no deciding — absolutely correct?

But how about the objection that just any belief, no matter how lunatic, can be justified, on the coherence view, because you can build a coherent web to include it? Coherence theorists often reply that it may not, in fact, be possible to create a suitably coherent system for any belief you name. The Flat-Earth example is a case in point. Despite all sorts of adjustments in other beliefs made necessary to include this belief in a coherent web, the whole is still very incoherent. Incoherencies pop up everywhere. For example: it's easy to confirm that the distance between New Zealand and Chile is about 6000 miles; yet, on the map produced by the Flat-Earthers, the two countries appear at opposite ends of the disc, so should be about 20,000 miles apart. A Flat-Earther might reply that this is something their scientists have yet to explain, and they'll get to work on it. Anomalies — inconsistencies and unexplained phenomena — show up in any belief system, of course. If they didn't show up in the conventionally accepted webs, then research scientists wouldn't have anything to do! Nevertheless, the Flat-Earth belief web shows little sign of ever achieving anything like an acceptable level of coherence. So the idea that you can build an acceptably coherent system to include just any belief might be wrong. Maybe there can't be more than one acceptably coherent web — ours.

The larger worry about coherentism, however, is that even if there is only one acceptably coherent web, then there's no assurance at all that a large number of beliefs in this web match reality. Coherence gives no assurance that *any* beliefs match reality.

Coherentists reply that beliefs aren't infallible, and that's something we're just going to have to live with. Foundationalists, they point out, run into the same problem of possible isolation from reality. Maybe our basic beliefs are actually not true, so large portions of the whole edifice built upon them, the beliefs foundationalists claim are justified, are in fact false.

Maybe you think that one of these two accounts of justification – foundationalism or coherentism – is better at facing this problem of possible isolation from reality. Anyway, the isolation possibility is one that is a very pervasive and familiar one in theory of knowledge.

We'll turn now from the question of the overall structure of the justification of knowledge to the question of where knowledge comes from.

6

A priori knowledge, analyticity and necessity

A priori/a posteriori

Where does knowledge come from? It's clear that some knowledge, at least, comes from perception. You might find out that the coffee cup is in front of you, that it's snowing outside, and that your dog is barking by seeing or otherwise perceiving these facts, that is, through sense-experience. Much of what you know by remembering it, or by relying on the testimony of what others have experienced, also ultimately depends on your sense-experience, or at least on somebody's. But a major topic for philosophical debate throughout all of the recorded history of philosophy has been about knowledge that doesn't ultimately depend on the senses. Philosophy has often considered this kind of knowledge: what sort it is, how extensive it is, and how to account for it.

Knowledge that depends on sensation is called **a posteriori** knowledge. This means, in Latin, *from afterwards* – after (that is, dependent upon) sense-experience. Knowledge that doesn't depend on sense-experience is called **a priori** knowledge, Latin for *from beforehand* – prior to (that is, independent of) sense-experience. The questions in this chapter are: what kinds of a priori knowledge are there? And how do we know that sort of thing? The answer to the second question is not obvious: how, after all, could you find out anything other than by using your senses?

Rationalism

Rationalism is the position that real knowledge, or at least important parts of it, are a priori.

Plato is a good example of a strong rationalist. He argued that what we sense – the everyday particulars that surround us – are, for several reasons, unsuitable objects for knowledge. Those everyday objects, he pointed out, are changeable (that cottage cheese in the back of the fridge is white and shiny today, but will be green and fuzzy in a few days), so any belief based on such things might be true at one time, false at another. Genuine knowledge must be unchanging, so what it's about must be eternal and unchanging. Further: what we sense in the everyday world varies according to its context, and according to the position and other characteristics of the person who apprehends them. (A six-year-old who's five feet tall looks very tall among his or her classmates, but short in a group of adults.) The resulting fluidity of belief based on the senses again makes it fall short of real knowledge. In addition: we can sense Fido, Rover, Lassie, Pluto, Scoobie-Doo, Snoopy, and so on, and learn about each individual dog through our senses, but what constitutes really significant knowledge is universal: what's true of all dogs, of dogs in general, of dogs just because they're dogs, the thing that makes them all dogs. And real knowledge must also be general in the sense of being about things that are timeless, not dated. My true belief that there was a full moon on 9 February, 2009, is too trivial and particular to count as real knowledge. And also: what our senses tell us is often not perfectly precise. You can always imagine that you could see better and more accurately, no matter how good your eyes (or glasses) are. This is not good enough to count as real knowledge. And last: what our senses tell us is sometimes wrong; it's always corrigible, dubitable, and fallible.

> Plato (c. 428–c. 347 BCE) was the ancient Greek philosopher who many consider the father of Western philosophy. He (and his teacher Socrates, and his student Aristotle) defined the problems and considered most of the solutions we've been considering ever since.

Plato (and many other philosophers) concluded that genuine knowledge could not be about everyday objects. It must be about a pure, unchanging, perfect realm of being; Plato's name for the objects inhabiting this realm has been translated as **forms** or **ideas**. There's one of them for every kind of thing: so there's one form for (e.g.) dogs. This has none of the variability, imperfection, or particularity of earthly dogs: it's the perfect, most general, pure form of doggyness, the ideal that no earthly dog comes very close to imitating, not even Best-In-Shows. These forms are invisible, unavailable to the senses: our contact with them must, then, be through pure understanding, a priori.

A good deal of this is not implausible. It does seem true that the best kind of knowledge is the most general, the least dependent on individual particular things and our observations of them. Scientific laws, after all, don't mention particular things or particular locations or times (some philosophers argue that laws are not allowed to), but rather concentrate on the most general sorts of facts – universal, we hope eternal, truths. And what scientists come up with is, we sometimes assume, superior in quality to what we ordinary folk believe.

But there are two pretty obvious problems with Plato's position. One is that, it seems, he's setting too high a standard for knowledge. Maybe some knowledge meets his high standards, but we count some everyday beliefs that don't meet those tests as knowledge too. We've already had a look at the somewhat similar position held by Descartes, and the similar criticism that might apply there. But maybe this is only a matter of how strict we want to be in awarding the prize of calling some belief 'knowledge'. Plato presumably had true and well-justified beliefs about, for example, where he left his left sandal last night, and presumably found this kind of thing to be valuable also, if not as exalted as what he got from contemplation of the eternal forms.

Other problems are more serious. The existence of a pure, unchangeable, invisible realm is of course questionable, and even if we accept this, there are difficulties in providing an account of how we know about what's there.

The epistemology of the a priori

Plato thought that a priori knowledge is **innate**, meaning inborn. This does not mean that we start believing what we know innately the moment we're born. (Some people, of course, never think about the truths of geometry which Plato thought were innate.) Plato meant that this sort of knowledge is latent within us, needing only the proper sort of stimulation to make it active. Once we're induced somehow to start thinking about it, we can come up with the right answers just by this thinking, without having to be taught them, or having to experience any evidence of them through our senses.

Some philosophers have called these beliefs *self-evident*. That doesn't mean that they count as evidence for themselves – that would be impossibly, uselessly circular; neither does it mean that they're simply obvious. It means that they (somehow) arrive with their own justification – they need nothing else to justify them. There still seems to be a mystery here.

Another traditional way of thinking about these beliefs is to say that we can arrive at them by our faculty of *rational intuition*. But that doesn't help much either. It seems that that's just a fancy way of saying that we come to them just by thinking about them, without needing sense-experience. It doesn't appear to help much in telling us what this kind of thought involves – that is, what makes it different from just guessing – or exactly why it's supposed to be reliable.

Descartes' story about a priori knowledge is that the method with which one arrives at a priori knowledge guarantees it: as long as our ideas are 'clear and distinct,' they're infallibly correct. He does make some attempt to explain what this clarity and distinctness is, and how to recognize it, but for our purposes, we can see it as the kind of understanding and belief you get when you contemplate self-evident basic truths, for example in arithmetic and geometry, or what you understand can be proven on their basis. When our beliefs come from perception, he argued, they're not clear and distinct, but rather fuzzy and confused, and we can refrain from believing what our senses indicate to us. But when our cognition is clear and distinct, belief is compelled.

But we want to ask him: can't you be mistaken about what beliefs are really clear and distinct? And even when you're correct, and the beliefs really are clear and distinct, why does that guarantee their truth? Why, in other words, is looking for clarity and distinctness any different from just guessing? In fact, Descartes asks himself these questions; his answer, disappointing to some philosophers, is that a benevolent God who created him wouldn't let him go wrong when he's doing his cognitive best.

Empiricism and the a priori

The historical alternative to rationalism is **empiricism.** The central tenet of this position is that important knowledge is all a posteriori; later, we'll talk about this. They usually do make some room for a priori knowledge – but it doesn't amount to anything important. A typical empiricist account of the a priori is David Hume's.

> **David Hume** (1711–76) was a Scottish philosopher and historian. He's sometimes thought to be the most important British philosopher of all time; certainly his influence has lasted for centuries. He's best known for his strong empiricism and the scepticism on various matters this sometimes implied.

Hume distinguished two kinds of knowledge, which he called 'relations of ideas' and 'matters of fact'. The first kind of knowledge is of truth which follows merely from the ideas that compose it. Examples of what we know this way are *All fathers are male* or *Triangles have three sides*. The negation of any of these, according to Hume, involves a self-contradiction; thus these facts have a sort of inevitability – they couldn't be otherwise. Matters of fact, by contrast, cannot be known merely by examining the relations of the ideas that compose such a judgment. To know that giraffes are vegetarians, for example, you (or someone) has to *observe* them. It's not a self-contradiction to suppose that there is a carnivorous giraffe. It takes observation to establish such truths, and it's always possible that observations show these propositions false. Propositions whose truth depends merely on the relations between the included ideas are mostly unimportant. Real knowledge *about the world* can't be gained merely by drawing out the logical consequences of the ideas in our mind: it has to be gained by observing it.

Rationalists were, of course, unimpressed by Hume's relegation of a priori knowledge to a very minor role. It seemed clear, contrary to Hume, that some sorts of a priori knowledge were knowledge about the world, substantial and important.

Consider the truth of geometry, for example, that the combined length of any two sides of a triangle is greater than the length of the third side. This, to all appearances, is neither a trivial matter, merely a result of the relations of ideas, nor something learned from sense-experience: just think about a triangle, and you'll realize it has to be true.

The resistance of some sorts of belief to any possible disproof by observation is a sign that such belief is a priori. Consider the belief that $5 + 7 = 12$. An extraordinary fact about this is that we refuse to count anything as observational evidence to the contrary. Consider these experiments:

> Dump five gallons of raisins into a bin. Add seven gallons of apples. Mix well. How many gallons of fruit result? The answer, of course, is not twelve gallons. It's pretty close to seven gallons, maybe a little over. The raisins are fitting in between the apples. The same sort of thing happens when you mix five gallons of alcohol with seven gallons of water: less than twelve gallons (but more than seven, and quite enough to have a big party).

Do these experiments show that sometimes $5 + 7 \neq 12$? No. Why not? Well, often people say that this isn't really *addition*. If it's really addition, $5 + 7$ will always be 12. Whenever observations appear to show that $5 + 7 \neq 12$, we'd always say that there was a mistake, or that what we were doing wasn't arithmetical adding.

The truths of geometry are similarly resistant to any proposed counter-evidence.

> At one point in high-school geometry class, we all took out our protractors – those little half-moon shaped things for measuring angles – and measured and added up the interior angles of a bunch of triangles we drew. The sums we got came to (something like) 173°, 184°, 178°, 192°, but never (or almost never) 180°.

Our geometry teacher did not conclude that we had made an important discovery contradicting what it said in the textbook. He told us instead that we had inaccurate protractors, and were guilty of inexact drawing, careless measurement, or faulty addition.

Here's another example:

> Your car alarm goes off often when the car's just parked and nobody's doing anything to it. You bring the car into the service station to have the mechanic find out what was wrong. The next day the car mechanic reports, 'I checked the alarm and electrical systems, and they're all perfect. There's no problem here.' So you ask, 'Well, what's causing the alarm to go off?' The mechanic replies, 'It just does. There isn't any reason.'

Even though you know a great deal less about how cars work than your mechanic does, in this case you know the mechanic is wrong. How do you know? Because *everything has a cause.* Nothing just happens, for no reason.

In all these cases, it seems, beliefs are immune to disproof from observational evidence, a sign of a priori knowledge.

What's still questionable, of course, is whether the a prioricity of these beliefs arises from the relation of ideas. On the face of it, however, this does not appear to be the case. They seem to be important truths about the world.

Necessity

It has commonly been assumed of truths known a priori that *they couldn't be otherwise.* No future observations – no *possible* observations – would make us count them false. But resistance to admitting observational evidence against a belief might not be a significant fact about the proposition believed; it might simply show the believer's psychological stubbornness, and the right reaction might be just to advise a bit of open-mindedness. But many philosophers believe that this stubbornness is the right policy in these cases, justified by the fact that in reality these facts *cannot* have exceptions, so any apparent counter-evidence *must* be mistaken. They're **necessary truths**. That doesn't mean that we can't do without them. That means that they have to be the way they are, that they could not be otherwise, no matter how the actual world is, was, will be, or might have been. Compare the other sort of truth: **contingent truth**. That my coffee cup is on the table in front of me is a contingent truth. It's true now, but it was false earlier, and will soon be false again. It might have been false even now: I might have taken it downstairs earlier (but I didn't). Contingent truths include more than particular matters depending on human action. They also include facts such as *this oak tree is 11 metres tall* and generalizations, such as *giraffes are vegetarians, Japan lies in an earthquake zone, on average it's colder in February the further north you go (in the northern hemisphere, at least)*. They even include consequences of the basic laws of science, and the laws themselves: *pigs can't fly* (a consequence of the facts about how pigs are built and the laws of aeronautics); *nothing can exceed the speed of light*. All contingent facts might have been otherwise – though it's hard, in some cases, to imagine an alternative world in which some of them are true. The idea here isn't psychological imaginability – it's supposed to be an objective matter which facts are necessary and which are merely contingent.

It's pretty clear why traditionally philosophers associated necessity with a prioricity. Necessary propositions don't depend on the way the world just happened to turn out – in other words, on the observable facts. Necessary truths would still be true even if the world looked, smelled (etc.) entirely different. So that's why, it's supposed, you don't need your senses to find out necessary truths. So how *do* you find out necessary truths?

Kant's epistemology of a prioricity

Kant, the great eighteenth-century Prussian philosopher, produced a revolutionary account of a priori knowledge, breaking with over twenty centuries of tradition, and influencing (though not convincing) everyone who considered the topic afterwards.

> Immanuel Kant (1724–1804) is considered by many to be the most important philosopher of the Enlightenment era, with enormous influence on future epistemology, metaphysics, and ethics. He attempted to combine empiricism and rationalism into an overarching theory that would establish the basis for empirical science and everyday knowledge.

According to Kant, a priori knowledge comes in two main varieties, which have to be understood very differently. The first variety is exactly what Hume called knowledge of relations-of-ideas. These can be known a priori, independently of experience – though experience might be necessary to give you the concepts involved in the first place. For example, you need experience to teach you the concepts of *father* and *male*. But once you have these concepts, then that's all it takes. You don't need additional experience to find out that all fathers are male. Compare a bit of clearly a posteriori knowledge: that giraffes are vegetarians. Experience is necessary to get the concept of *giraffe*, and of *vegetarian*, but having these concepts isn't sufficient for knowledge that giraffes are vegetarians. Knowledge of this depends on observation.

A concept, as we're going to be thinking about it, is an ability – the ability to sort things out in a particular way. The concept *male*, for example, is the ability to sort things out into those that are males and those that aren't. The concept *tamarind* is the ability to distinguish between tamarinds and non-tamarinds. I don't have that concept – I haven't a clue what tamarinds are, and couldn't pick one out from other things.

Some concepts are (roughly speaking) built out of others. You might think of the concept *father* as built from two other concepts: *parent* and *male*. We can imagine, then, that the reason you're able to sort things into fathers and non-fathers when you have the concept *father* is that you've understood the concepts it's built out of. So to do the sorting involved in applying the concept *father*, you might sort things into parents and non-parents, and then, in the parent pile, sort those items out into males and females. Then the males in the parent pile are fathers.

This offers a way to understand the example of a priori knowledge we've been looking at. Suppose that having a concept – being able to sort in that particular way – involves knowing the concepts that are 'built' into it, and being able to sort using them. So having the concept *father* is having the concepts *male* and *parent*, and knowing that both must apply for something to count as a father. That's why all you have to have is the concept father, and then you automatically know that anything that's a father is male.

What we've done here is to construct a version of Kant's account of one form of a priori knowledge. Kant used the word **'analytic'** for this kind of proposition because he found an analogy here with *analysis*, which means taking something apart into its components. The truth of 'All fathers are male' can be determined merely by taking the concept *father* apart into its components, and seeing that the concept male is already contained in it.

Kant called propositions that weren't analytic **synthetic**. These are exactly what Hume called matters-of-fact. A synthetic proposition, in Kant's way of thinking about it, is made of concepts that do not have this sort of containment relation: one is not included in the other. They're two distinct concepts, put together in the proposition. The analogy here is with the idea of *synthesis*, which means putting different things together. So for example, the proposition that giraffes are vegetarians is a synthetic proposition, because the predicate concept, *vegetarian*, is not contained within the subject concept, *giraffes*. That's why you can understand all the constituent concepts involved in that proposition, but not thereby automatically know that the proposition is true.

> The subject of a sentence is what or whom the sentence is about: in 'Giraffes are vegetarian' it's 'giraffes'. The predicate is the part of the sentence that tells something about the subject: 'are vegetarian'.

Consider the following true propositions. All of them would be good candidates for analyticity, but only the first one seems obviously to be a case of Kantian 'containment':

1 Ice is frozen water.
2 A metre contains 100 centimetres.
3 If Felicity lives next-door to Sid, then Sid lives next-door to Felicity.
4 If Mildred is taller than Norton, then Norton is shorter than Mildred.
5 It's Tuesday or it's not Tuesday.

Maybe sentences 2–5 could be explained in terms of 'containment', maybe not. What exactly is involved in conceptual containment? Kant illustrated his account with an example:

> If I say 'All bodies are extended', this is an analytic judgment. To find that extension is connected with the concept that I link with the word 'body', I don't need to go beyond that concept; all I need do is to analyse it, i.e. become conscious of the

manifold [something that's complex, with many parts or elements] that I always think when I have a thought of *body* – and then I'll find *in* it the concept of extension. If on the other hand I say 'All bodies are heavy', this is a synthetic judgment: its predicate is not a *part* of what is involved in my general thought of *body*; it is being *added* to the subject, which is what makes this a synthetic judgment.

Is this helpful? What do *you* always find when you think about *body*? Do you find having weight as part of this concept? I do. I remember having the concept of *physical object* (what Kant means by 'body') defined for me by my high school teacher as anything that takes up space *and has weight*. Maybe your concept of physical object is vague enough so that there's no answer to the question whether it includes the idea of having weight or not. The problem here is that if you rely on what people are conscious of when they think about their concepts, you might come up with different answers – in fact, with just about any answer. Little Timmy thinks of *all* men (males above a certain age) as fathers – because the men he's encountered so far have been somebody's father. That's *his* concept of father. I think of a grey short-haired animal when I think *cat*, because my former cat was like that, but clearly 'Cats are grey' is not analytic. Obviously, you can't rely on what anyone happens to find involved in their thinking. Kant would be the first to agree that what makes a proposition analytic must be an objective matter having to do with truth and justification, and not dependent on the quirks of anyone's psychology or experience.

Kant also remarks that in distinguishing the analytic from the synthetic he is guided (like Hume, as we saw) by the idea that the denial of an analytic statement is a self-contradiction, while the denial of a synthetic statement is not. 'It's raining and it's not raining' is clearly a self-contradiction, asserting and denying the same thing, but 'It's false that all fathers are male' is not a self-contradiction in this clear way.

The synthetic a priori

Despite some problems in Kant's way of explaining the analytic/synthetic distinction, both it, and Kant's view that belief that analytic propositions constitute one form of a priori knowledge, have received considerable acceptance among philosophers since. What's much more controversial, however, and much more important to Kant's overall philosophy, is his view that only *some* a priori knowledge is a result of the analyticity of the proposition. There is also a priori knowledge of synthetic propositions. This is where he significantly departed from Hume's empiricism.

You can see why this position is more surprising. We have something like an intuitive idea of *concept inclusion*, Kant's account of how analyticity produces a priori knowledge: you know in advance that anything you're going to count as a father will be male, because being male is one of the things you look for in classifying something as a father. But it's much harder to see how one can know a synthetic proposition a priori. The truth of a synthetic proposition does not follow merely from the nature of the subject and predicate concepts. How can there be synthetic a priori knowledge?

But first we should ask: is there any such thing? Kant tried to prove the existence of synthetic a priori knowledge by producing examples. Among the examples of a priori knowledge we considered earlier, *All fathers are male* is pretty clearly analytic; but others are cases Kant would count as synthetic. He argued, for example, that you can't discover that $5 + 7 = 12$ is true by analysing the concepts involved. 'When I have the thought of the sum of 5 and 7, I do *not* thereby have the thought of 12; no matter how long I spend analysing my concept of such a possible sum, I won't find 12 in it.' Similarly, he argued that the proposition that every change has a cause can't be discovered by analysis: the concept of change and the concept of cause are independent − neither is included in the other.

So how do we know these (supposedly) synthetic a priori truths? Kant argued that these truths are the *presuppositions* of our experience of the world and our knowledge of it. What this means is that their truth is a precondition of our knowing anything. For example, the way we experience the world as spread out in space and time presupposes the truths of mathematics and geometry; that is, the only way a mind could experience and think about them is in terms of the concepts and properties and relations of number and figure that constitute mathematics and geometry. As a result, we know in advance that any objects we observe will obey the laws of mathematics and geometry. Similarly, we know in advance that every change has a cause, because this 'principle of causality' is the only possible framework for our scientific or everyday experience and thought about things.

Here's an analogy: suppose that you always wore blue sunglasses. You'd know in advance that everything would look blue, not because that's the way it really is, but because that's the only way you'd see it. This analogy is not a perfect one for Kant's view, however: if you took those sunglasses off, you'd see things in their real colours, but in Kant's view, what we impose on any contact with the world cannot be removed – it's the only way any rational mind could apprehend anything. So there isn't any way that things would seem to be to us without these ways of encountering it. The 'world in itself' – how it is independently of these imposed ways of apprehending it – is something we certainly can't know anything about – can't even think about. The only way we can think about things is in those terms that make things thinkable to us! That's why we know in advance that anything that we think about will conform to those terms. When the mind considers itself, it can discover the structures it must impose on all its experience. That's where it gets its synthetic a priori knowledge.

There's a certain plausibility in Kant's idea that our pre-existing mental structure forms all our experience and thought; problems arise, however, in Kant's attempt to prove that the particular structures he talks about are necessary for any mind. Might it not be possible for us to experience and understand things in other ways?

Empiricism after Kant

Post-Kant empiricists devoted considerable energy to refuting his views, objecting most notably to his belief in the existence of the synthetic a priori. Following Hume, they took the only kind of necessary proposition, and the only kind knowable a priori, to be analytic propositions. What they had to do, then, was to try to show that Kant's proposed examples of the synthetic a priori were either not synthetic or not a priori.

John Stewart Mill, continuing the tradition of British empiricism, claimed that the truths of arithmetic and geometry were synthetic, but contingent and a posteriori, just like any other generalizations of science. He argued that propositions such as *5 + 7 = 12* and *The shortest distance between two points is a straight line* seem to be necessary and a priori because they are so completely obvious, having been observed to be true so frequently. The impression that these aren't learned from experience arises because the experiences we learned them from happened very early in our lives, long forgotten. We won't let anything count as empirical counter-evidence because these

John Stewart Mill (1806–73) was an influential English philosopher well known as the systematizer and popularizer of the doctrine of Utilitarianism, a moral and political theory. But he was also an empiricist epistemologist.

generalizations are so extremely well corroborated by countless past experiences that they can't be overturned by any isolated and minor apparent counter-instances.

But the apparent necessity, generality, and independence of empirical confirmation of (at least some of) Kant's examples made Mill's approach seem implausible to many empiricists; they preferred to count these propositions analytic, as Hume claimed. But what was needed was a better account than Kant's of the analytic/synthetic distinction. You'll recall he had two accounts of the analytic proposition: that it was one whose predicate concept was contained in its subject concept; and one whose denial was a self-contradiction. Neither of these seemed to do the job. The idea of conceptual containment was too psychological – too suggestive of the subjective and variable – and also vague and metaphorical, insufficiently explicit about how it was to be detected. And to say that the denial of an analytic proposition was a self-contradiction wasn't helpful either. 'It's not the case that all fathers are male' might be in some sense a self-contradiction, but it isn't an *explicit* self-contradiction, in the way 'There is a male who isn't a male' or 'It's Tuesday and it's not Tuesday' would be.

Around the turn of the twentieth century many philosophers decided that a much more promising way to approach analyticity would be to distinguish analytic and synthetic *sentences*, not propositions. An analytic truth, according to this new way of looking at things, is (very roughly speaking) a sentence that is true just because of the meanings of the words in it. This is the **linguistic theory of analyticity**.

More particularly, here's the suggestion made by Gottlob Frege. In an 1884 publication, Frege argued that analyticity could be rigorously detected using the notions of logical truth and synonyms. A **logical truth** is a sentence that's true merely because of the logical words in it – words such as 'all', 'no', 'and', 'or'. These are the words in the sentence other than the referring terms such as 'fathers', 'male', 'vegetarians', 'giraffes'. Logical truths are true sentences that remain true no matter what referring terms are uniformly substituted. 'All ducks are ducks' is true, and so is 'All wombats are wombats' and 'All cyclotrons are cyclotrons', and so on; so all these are logical truths. They're made true by the meanings of the logical words involved, given the particular structure they give to the sentences they're in. All you have to know, in order to know the truth of such sentences, is the meaning of the logical words inside: once you understand the logical framework, 'All _____ are _____ ', you will see that putting the same referring term into both blanks

> Gottlob Frege (1848–1925) was a German mathematician, logician, and philosopher. His work was pivotal in the production of contemporary logic as a formal system – the first major overhaul since Aristotle.

will automatically be true, no matter what the world is like. Thus we have an explanation of why logical truths, anyway, are a priori.

Frege argued as well that mathematical truths were a form of logical truth. This would make the truths of arithmetic (and of mathematics in general) analytic.

Logical truths are only one species of analytic truth. If the explanation above works, then we're still left with explaining analytic truths such as 'Every father is male'. Frege's explanation here is that sentences like this can be converted into logical truths by substituting synonyms for one or more of the referring terms. Thus in the sentence 'Every father is male' we substitute for 'father' the synonymous 'male parent' and get the logical truth 'Every male parent is male.' (That is, all sentences created by appropriate substitutions are true: 'Every green duck is green', 'Every unfunny joke is unfunny', and so on.

Here's one problem with Frege's view. It depends crucially

on the notion of the logical form of a sentence for his definition, but this is not merely a matter of its grammatical form. The grammatical form 'All XYs are Ys' does not always represent the logical form that makes the sentences above logical truths. 'All white ducks are ducks' is logically true, but 'All decoy ducks are ducks' is not. It has the same grammatical form, but not the same logical form, as the other sentence. Specification of the logical forms of sentences, and of methods for telling what the form of a sentence is, turns out to be an extremely difficult problem.

Empiricists on the a priori

Many twentieth-century empiricists had a more complicated view, seeing mathematics and geometry as either analytic a priori, or synthetic a posteriori, depending on what sort of arithmetic and geometry you're talking about. This needs explanation.

First, consider the notion of an **uninterpreted calculus**. (The word 'calculus' here merely means *system for calculating*, not the particular branch of mathematics called 'the calculus'). This is, in essence, a systematic game played with a bunch of invented symbols, according to a bunch of invented rules. You write things down using combinations of these symbols, and if they follow the rules for combining the symbols, then they can be judged 'true' or 'false' by applying other rules. Obeying the rules – in some cases, being derivable using them – is all it takes, and all it means, to be 'true'. But all this has nothing to do with the real world outside the game. If we understand these rules as defining the symbols used in the game, then the true or false symbol-combinations are true or false merely by definition. What we get, then, is solely analytic truth or falsity.

But now suppose you add to this uninterpreted calculus a set of correspondence rules, which tell you how to *interpret* the symbols – how to understand them as referring to things and their relations in the real world. Roughly speaking, then, pure mathematics is an uninterpreted calculus; applied mathematics an **interpreted calculus**. An interpreted calculus makes claims about the real world; but now there are questions about whether each statement made in it is true or false. This has to be determined by observation. So the statements in an interpreted calculus are synthetic and a posteriori. What we're always on the lookout for, of course, is ways to come up with true beliefs about the real world. So interpretations which yield false statements are discarded, and other ones tried.

This view appears to make sense of our earlier stories about empirical tests of arithmetic and geometry. In the experiment in which we added apples and raisins, putting stuff into a big container, mixing, and measuring was an interpretation of the symbols of arithmetic that yielded false (synthetic a posteriori) statements. But because we presumably want to use arithmetic

Here's an interesting historical example of the surprising empirical test results of an interpreted geometry. A natural interpretation of a straight line in geometry is the path a beam of light follows. (You can tell whether a ruler is fairly straight by sighting down it.) With this interpretation would Euclidian geometry yield true statements? Einstein's physics predicted that very large – astronomical – triangles made from beams of light would have interior angles that totalled slightly but measurably more than 180°, and observations during an eclipse in 1919 showed that he was right. That means either you need to find a different interpretation, to make thus-interpreted Euclidian geometry true, or (and this is the reaction scientists preferred) you can reject Euclidian geometry as the calculus for measuring space, and use instead a much more easily interpreted geometry in which, for example, the sum of the angles of a triangle is always greater than 180° – a non-Euclidian geometry.

in the real world, we discard this interpretation, and try to find interpretations that happen to turn out true. When the uninterpreted calculus of geometry was interpreted in a way so that 'straight line' meant those messy things we drew with pencil and ruler, and 'size of an angle' meant the very rough readings we got with our protractor, then the interpreted statements came out false. If we wanted to use this uninterpreted calculus for real-world application, then we should instead have found an interpretation that made them come out true.

If this general picture of mathematics and geometry is right, what becomes of Kant's argument that the only way to see reality is via their truths? First, we have to say that, as uninterpreted calculi, the propositions of ordinary mathematics and geometry are hardly inevitable: you can cook up any sort of uninterpreted calculus you like. But as tools for understanding real observed phenomena, uninterpreted propositions need interpretation, and given some interpretations they come out false (so they're hardly necessarily true). As for his assertion that the propositions of ordinary mathematics and geometry are the only frameworks in which the rational mind can approach the external world, the existence of alternatives (for example, non-Euclidian geometry) which rational people actually sometimes use appears to prove this wrong.

Quine on the analytic/synthetic distinction

By the middle of the twentieth century, empiricists were convinced that they had managed to produce a satisfactory (Humean) account of all those areas of knowledge that Kant took to be synthetic a priori. But in 1951, the rug was pulled out from under them by a widely read and hugely influential article by W. V. O. Quine, which many took to demolish the analytic/

synthetic distinction. The main argument in Quine's article is that there is no good explanation of what that distinction is supposed to be.

Frege's explanation relies, as we've seen, on the notions of logical form and synonymy. Quine argues that neither notion holds water. Our rough-and-ready idea of logical form – the structure of the sentence due to the logical words – is not, according to Quine, a clear notion. Which are the logical words? The answer we've given, which gives a list of them, is not philosophically sufficient. What makes those words *logical* words?

Neither does Quine accept the idea of synonymy. How could this idea be explained? You might propose that when two words are synonymous you can replace one by the other in any sentence without changing the sentence's *truth-value*, that is, without changing it from true to false, or vice versa; but that's not right, because it's the case with merely *co-extensive* terms, that is, terms that just happen to refer to the same thing. Quine's example is 'renates' (creatures with kidneys) and 'cordates' (creatures with a heart). Anything you say that's true about renates would also be true of cordates, because, in fact, everything that has a heart has kidneys. And everything that is false about one is false about the other. Well, then, let's try to explain synonymy as what we can replace in sentences claiming that something is *necessary*: it's necessary that cordates have a heart, but it's not necessary that renates have a heart – it just happens to be that way as a matter of biological fact. But what does 'necessary' mean? What makes 'cordates have a heart' necessary? Well, it's true by virtue of the meanings of the words – analytic. We're back where we started, and no progress has been made.

Quine's critics sometimes agreed that explanations of synonymy formed a circle, but pointed out that this is often a feature of explanations of legitimate concepts. And the notion of analyticity surely seems legitimate. Don't you (they asked Quine) recognize the distinction between the reason why 'Podiatrists are physicians that specialize in the foot' is true, and the reason why 'Podiatrists are less numerous than general practitioners' is true? One is true by definition, the other one isn't. Quine's reply is that yes, he recognizes a distinction between the two sentences, but it isn't that one is true by virtue of meaning alone and the other one isn't. It's merely that one (the first) is closer to the centre of our 'web of belief' (which we discussed in an earlier chapter), meaning that it's more resistant to revision based on new evidence of our senses. In other words it's, relatively speaking, more a priori, less a posteriori, than the other sentence. That's the substance of their difference, according to Quine.

Quine, then, denies that there is a sensible notion of 'meaning' that can figure in 'meaning the same' or 'true by virtue of meaning'. By consequence, he argued that there is no analytic/synthetic distinction, and thus no explanation of a prioricity based on analyticity. He does accept the a priori/a posteriori distinction, but he argues that this is not a clear-cut black/white matter. It's a matter of degree. Every sentence, to some extent or other, could be rejected as false if subjected to enough contrary evidence from our senses, but some sentences are relatively more a priori in that they are relatively more resistant to that kind of rejection. This implies that sentences like 'Every father is male' might be rejected based on contrary evidence; they're relatively a priori, meaning that they're relatively resistant to contrary evidence, but not (as we assumed in the previous chapter) completely immune. This, of course, seems quite implausible, maybe even unintelligible. On the pre-Quine view, were a huge amount of unexpected evidence to result in our starting to count some fathers as female, we'd see this as a change in the meaning of the words, rather than a change in belief. But Quine argues that there is, at base, no way of distinguishing between these two.

Necessity again

Quine's attack on the linguistic theory of analyticity is the best known and most influential criticism; but other philosophers have occasionally been unhappy with that theory too. A very basic criticism some recent philosophers have made is this one. What makes a sentence true is that it corresponds to a fact out there in the world. The meanings of the words in the sentence determine what facts would make it true, but they can't, all by themselves, *make* it true. The real reason why 'All white ducks are ducks' is true is not its meaning, but the fact that white ducks *are* ducks. Nevertheless there is a difference between 'All white ducks are ducks' and 'All white ducks live near water.' Both are true, but only one is necessarily true – couldn't be otherwise; this is a consequence of a difference between the facts that they correspond to: the fact that all ducks are ducks is a necessary fact; the fact that all ducks live near water is only a contingent fact. We shouldn't mistake this difference in the kind of fact referred to for a difference in the way the meanings are arranged in the sentences.

Quine would not be happy with the criticism of the linguistic theory of the analytic we've just looked at. It claims that what's taken to be the analytic/synthetic distinction is really the necessary/contingent distinction; but Quine is just as critical of the second distinction as he is of the first, and for something like the same reasons. Necessary truths are traditionally conceived of as those that could not be otherwise; so if we correctly apprehend a proposition as being necessarily true, then we should take that belief as immune from revision. But Quine, as we've seen, argues that no belief is like this. Experiences incompatible with that belief can arise for any belief, and, given enough of these experiences, it can become rational to reject any belief.

This is not to say, however, that all beliefs are on a par. As we've seen earlier, Quine holds that some beliefs are so

entrenched in our web that it would take a great deal of apparently contrary experience to overturn them. These are the ones,
according to Quine, that we misleadingly call necessary (or a
priori). This is not an arbitrary matter. One way entrenchment
happens is when that belief is a 'natural necessity' – a law of
nature – a very well-established generalization, central to the
theory of some science. Another way entrenchment can happen
is when a belief is so obvious that we would rather discount the
veracity of contrary evidence than reject it. (Recall, here, Mill's
position.) These 'necessities' are matters of degree: the propositions which we believe in can have various degrees of recalcitrance to revision. And the source of this recalcitrance is not, for
Quine, what some traditions in philosophy had thought it to be:
logical, conceptual, or linguistic. We learn the necessity of this
sort of generalization the way we learn everything: by ordinary
observation, and by the sophisticated observation that constitutes
science.

The biggest difference between Quine's view and the traditional one (which still has many adherents) is that tradition takes
necessity to be a metaphysical property: that is, something that's
true (or false) of facts or propositions. In Quine's analysis,
however, it's more like an epistemological property – resistance
to revision. It's a matter simply of how unwilling we'd be to take
apparent contrary evidence to merit revision.

Quine's view that no belief is immune from revision extends
even to the laws of logic. One of these is the Law of Non-
Contradiction, which has two versions: (1) For any proposition
p, it's not the case that both p and not-p; (2) For any individual
thing x, and any property P, it's not the case that both x has P
and x has not-P. (So it's not the case that it's Tuesday and it's
not Tuesday; and it's not the case that anything is both green and
not-green.) In his 1953 article 'Two Dogmas of Empiricism',
the one we've been referring to, Quine appears to be willing to
allow that even this law might be given up were there a great

deal of contrary evidence – though clearly that possibility is very far-fetched. A lot of philosophers have found this extremely implausible: it's inconceivable that anything could cast doubt on this law, isn't it? Maybe Quine himself came around to agree. In later writings, he appeared to have relented on the extreme position of unrevisability, and fallen back, in a limited way, on the view that logical laws, at least, are analytic, guaranteed true by the meanings of the logical words involved, so that anyone who appeared to disagree must be using the logical words differently – must be speaking a different language.

The traditional and revisionist epistemologies of necessity

The traditional view (till a couple of decades ago) was that necessary propositions are known only a priori, and contingent propositions only a posteriori. Here's why these views have seemed reasonable. Sense-experience, it seems, can tell you only what is actually the case, not what's necessarily the case – what *is* true, not what *must be* true. So it appears that you can't find out necessary truths by means of the senses – that is, a posteriori. If knowledge of necessary truths is possible at all, it must be a priori. Pure thought or reasoning or intuition (or whatever you take to be the a priori method for justifying belief) would seem powerless to tell us what the actual world is like. It might tell us necessary truths, what's true of any possible world, but it can't tell us contingent truths – what just happens to be true of *this* world. So knowledge of contingent truths can't be had a priori. It must be a posteriori.

But recently some philosophers have argued against this traditional view. The most famous arguments are due to Saul Kripke. Against the view that everything known a priori is necessary, he uses the example of the standard metre bar. This metal bar kept in Paris under carefully controlled conditions had marks on it setting the international standard for the length of one metre. (This is no longer the standard, but we'll ignore this and pretend it still is.) Now, consider the proposition that the distance between those marks on that bar is one metre long. You know that a priori – after all, those marks *stipulate* the metre. But

> Saul Kripke, born in 1940, is a philosopher and logician based at Princeton University. His book *Naming and Necessity*, published in 1972, caused something like a revolution in philosophy, causing large-scale rethinking in the philosophy of language, and restoring metaphysics to the important place in English-language philosophy it had lost over the previous decades.

this proposition is contingent. It's not necessary that those lines are one metre apart. Imagine, for example, that the temperature control breaks down, and the metre bar heats up and expands. Then those marks would be a little further apart than one metre.

That's supposed to be an example of a contingent proposition known a priori; but here's an example he argues is a necessary proposition known a posteriori: *water is* H_2O. It's clear, first, that this is known a posteriori, and only that way. Nobody knew it until observations made by scientists demonstrated it. Kripke's controversial claim is that this is necessary. Perhaps the following will convince you: imagine what would be the case if the colourless, tasteless liquid that fills ponds and rivers and is mixed with Scotch were not H_2O, but had some other chemical composition – call it XYZ. Were that the case, then what fills ponds and rivers and what's mixed with Scotch would not be water – it would be some other compound. If it weren't H_2O, then it wouldn't be water. It's necessary that water is H_2O. (But on the contrary, it might be argued that this *would* then be water – it's just that then water would have turned out to be XYZ, not H_2O.)

Possible worlds

There's a peculiar sort of process that's become currently
generally acceptable for discovering what's necessary, what's
contingent, and what's impossible. It appears to be a priori.
Here's how it works.

Central to this process is the idea of a *possible world*. To
understand this, imagine first a list – a long list – of all the facts
there are. That collection of facts constitutes the *real* world. It
includes the fact that at 9 pm on 16 February, 2009, it was -1°
C in Cincinnati, along with a whole lot of other facts. Now
imagine a slightly different world, where everything else was the
same (as much as possible) but the temperature was -2° C in
Cincinnati then. That's a different possible world, a merely
possible, not actual, world.

Why did I say, 'as much as possible'? Why can't you have an
imaginary world just like this one except for just that one difference? One reason is that if the laws of nature are the same as in
this world, there would have had to be slightly different conditions slightly earlier than that time, resulting in a slightly lower
temperature. But there would also have had to have been different causes of those conditions, and so on back. It seems that if
we want our imaginary possible world to have our laws of
nature, then we'd have to include a very large number of different facts. (A leading theorist of possible-world-thought argues,
controversially, that the possible world closest to the actual one
is just like this one in its history, but with one factual difference
plus a slight change in the laws of nature to produce this one
difference given the same past as ours.)

So that's one possible world. (Really, it's two: the real world
is a possible world, and the very close possible but not actual one
we've just described is another.) Imagine other large or small
changes from the real world, and you've got other possible
worlds. Impossible worlds are ones that are logically inconsis-

tent: like ones in which Joanna's birthday this year is on Tuesday, and it's not on Tuesday.

This idea provides the material for defining necessary, contingent, and impossible propositions. The necessary ones are true in all possible worlds. The contingent truths are true in the actual world, as well as some (but not all) other possible worlds. The contingent falsehoods are false in the actual world, but true in some (but not all) other possible worlds. The impossible ones are false in every possible world.

But this does not give us an epistemology for necessity and possibility. How do we know that some true propositions are necessary, and others only contingent (that is, true but possibly false)? It doesn't help just to say that a necessary proposition is true not just in this world, but in all possible worlds (and to give the other definitions above). How do we know what other possible worlds are like? Kripke, the originator of the contemporary possible-world interpretation for necessity and possibility, says that possible worlds are not like foreign countries you can visit, or distant places you might see through a powerful enough telescope. In other words, facts about necessity and possibility are not discovered empirically. For him, possible worlds are imaginary places, not real. You *stipulate* what happens there, you don't *discover* it. So, for example, because our intuitions tell us that it's possible that water freeze at 10° C instead of 0° C, we stipulate that there are some possible worlds where it freezes at 10° C. But because our intuitions tell us that it's necessary that water is H_2O, we stipulate that there are no possible worlds where it isn't. This looks very much like an a priori procedure. But where do we get these intuitions? Are they *true*? We appear to be back where we've started, with the old problem of providing an epistemology for the a priori.

7

Knowledge based on sense-experience

The central view of empiricism, as we have seen, is that sense-experience is the major − or only − source of real knowledge. Through much of history, it wasn't a popular position. Many philosophers agreed with Plato and Descartes that sense-experience was not the source of genuine (or important) knowledge. But from the seventeenth century onward empiricism became a much more mainstream view; the simultaneous rise of empiricism and modern science is no coincidence. Many − perhaps most − philosophers have incorporated some or much empiricism into their views ever since.

Among the ancients, Aristotle (384–322 BCE) and Epicurus (341–270 BCE), especially the latter, show empiricist tendencies, though there are significant rationalist tendencies in Aristotle, and ambiguities, gaps, and lapses of clarity in the positions of both. Thomas Aquinas (c. 1225–74) espoused empiricism of a sort, which he thought he got from Aristotle. But empiricism came into its own during the seventeenth and eighteenth centuries, with Thomas Hobbes (1588–1679) and the group of three philosophers known as the British Empiricists. John Locke (1632–1704), was the first of these; his theory of knowledge was strongly influential, though he's probably better known today for his political philosophy. The others, who refined Locke's epistemology and ironed out some inconsistencies, were George Berkeley (1685–1753) and David Hume.

Empiricism about concepts

The empiricist slogan, credited to Aristotle and repeated often afterwards, is 'Nothing in the intellect not previously in the senses.' This can mean at least two important but different things. The first way that slogan might be interpreted is that there are no *concepts* that arise other than from experience. A concept, you'll recall, as we're using that notion, is merely the ability to sort things a certain way. The second way is that there are no *beliefs* that arise other than from experience. Concepts are (putting it loosely) ingredients of beliefs: the belief that the dog is on the log 'contains' so to speak the concepts *dog* and *log* (and maybe other concepts too, such as *being on*), but this set of concepts does not add up to the belief. They have to be combined in a certain way and affirmed by the mind.

John Locke, in his important epistemological work *An Essay Concerning Human Understanding*, distinguishes between two sorts of what he calls 'simple ideas' – what we might call 'basic concepts'. They are *ideas of sensation* and *ideas of reflection*. The first are concepts of characteristics detected by the senses; Locke's examples are 'yellow, white, heat, cold, soft, hard, bitter, sweet'. The second are concepts of characteristics detected by introspection, 'the perception of the operations of our own mind within us ... And such are perception, thinking, doubting, believing, reasoning, knowing, willing.' Locke thought of both types of idea as derived from 'experience' in the larger sense, including inward experience of the operations of one's own mind.

In addition to these simple concepts there are complex ones, combinations of simple ones. These come only indirectly from experience, according to Locke. You get the simple concepts *purple* and *cow* from experience of purple things and cows, but the complex concept *purple cow* is invented by you, by combining these two concepts; it's not derived from experience of purple cows, which you've never seen (and never hope to see).

Locke's *Essay* argues against 'the received doctrine, that men have native ideas, and original characters, stamped upon their minds in their very first being'. The position he's opposed to is often called the doctrine of **innate ideas.** Locke argues that 'children and idiots' appear not to have certain concepts, and that prior to having sense-experiences associated with concepts, we can detect no such concept in our minds. Plato, a clear proponent of conceptual innatism, would have no problem with this supposed evidence against innate concepts. His position is that these ideas are always in one's mind, but that one needs some intellectual maturity, and sometimes some educational prodding, before these latent ideas can come into awareness. Locke firmly rejects the idea that there can be something in one's mind that one is unaware of, though his view would be hard to defend. There are all sorts of examples which seem to be instances of mental contents not the subject of active mental awareness. Concepts you're not actively thinking about are in some sense in your mind all the while. You probably didn't have a single thought about Bolivia yesterday, but the concept was there all that time. It seems clear, however, that the origin of that (and many another) concept had to be in sense-experience: someone who had no experience at all (the experience of being in Bolivia, or of hearing or reading about it) could hardly have had that concept.

How are we to tell, then, whether Locke or Plato is right? Does the prodding of education elicit latent, innate concepts (for example, of arithmetic) or does it teach them brand-new? The main sort of argument in favour of the conceptual-innateness hypothesis involves providing examples of concepts which, it's claimed, *could not be learned* from experience. Innatists have offered concepts such as the following:

Any **general concept**. The concept you have of your dog Fido
is a particular concept, no doubt the product of your
sense-experience. The concept you have of *dog*, on the other
hand, is a general concept.

The idea of causality

Religious ideas, e.g., God, soul

Ethical concepts, e.g., good, evil

The concepts of mathematics

The basic structural concepts that constitute the form of
language

Empiricists' replies come in two varieties:

1   They try to show that these concepts are complex, composed
of simple concepts which originated from sensation; or
2   They argue that these are not real concepts at all.

We'll look at a small sample of these debates.

Empiricism and general concepts

You'd think that it's obvious that you get the general concept
dog from having seen a number of dogs (or pictures
of dogs, descriptions of dogs, and so on). But Plato argued that
individual experiences are not sufficient to produce general
concepts. Having the concept *dog* means being able to classify a
wide variety of dogs into that category – knowing what dogness
in general involves. But seeing particular dogs never gives you
this information. All you know from your senses is Fido, Rover,
Spot, and so on – not the General Dog. This is one of his reasons
for claiming that our senses – our perceptions of the sense-
perceivable – cannot account for our concepts.

Empiricists recognized that the origin of general concepts
was a problem for them. Locke agreed that seeing Fido and
some other dogs was not in itself sufficient to form the concept

dog. Each individual dog-perception creates a different particular dog-idea; but then the mind has to use these particular perceptions to construct the concept, by a process he called *abstraction*. Having seen several dogs, what you do is somehow recognize the similarities in all of them, and use them to construct the general idea of dog-ness.

Berkeley didn't like this. He shared the empiricist view that ideas are copies of sense-experience. So when you see Rover, you have a particular visual impression of Rover, and later when you remember this experience, you have an idea of Rover, which is a copy of this original visual impression that see in your mind's eye. Because every idea must be a copy of some particular sense-impression, he argued against the existence of general concepts, which he called 'abstract ideas':

> Whatever hand or eye I imagine, it must have some particular shape and colour. Likewise the idea of man that I frame to myself must either be of a white, or a black, or a tawny, a straight, or a crooked, a tall, or a low, or a middle-sized man. I cannot by any effort of thought conceive the abstract idea described above.

But, of course, Berkeley recognized that we do need to think and talk about things in general – about dogs in general, not just about Fido or Spot. (When you decide that you want to get a dog, it might be that you're not picturing any particular colour or shape of dog.) Further, we need to identify any number of things as falling into a category *dog*. Unless we had abstract general ideas, how could we do it? Berkeley's own answer is somewhat less than satisfying. Each individual dog is associated with its own particular idea, but then each of these ideas is associated with each other. So your idea of Fido, so to speak, has a note attached to it saying, 'See also the idea of Rover, the idea of Spot' (and so on). The problem here is that we perform this association, but then what? We're still left with the original problem. We've got a bunch of mental images of particular dogs, but how are these to be used to identify Rex, whom we've never seen before, as a dog, given that he doesn't exactly match any of the cross-referenced particular dog-concepts? And to identify Felix (the cat) as a non-dog, given that he matches in some respects a number of the cross-referenced dog-concepts? Maybe these questions can be answered, but asking them shows that Berkeley's minimal view of the contents and actions of the mind isn't alone sufficient to account for concepts.

Hume didn't like the idea of general ideas either, and wanted to populate the mind only with particular ideas. So how do we think about dogs in general, or decide that Rex, a newly observed critter, is one of them? What you do, according to Hume, is retrieve a stored particular idea, a picture in the mind's eye of a particular dog and associated with the name 'dog', and compare it to the sense-impression at hand; given sufficient similarity, you'll recognize Rex as meriting the name 'dog' also; and Felix's cat-impressions as dissimilar enough not to be included. But again this is insufficient. Suppose your particular dog-image represents something hairy, four-legged, barking, brown, facing right, with tongue hanging out. But Rex is hairy, four-legged, not barking, white, facing left, with tongue hanging out. And Felix is also hairy, four-legged, facing right, but not brown, not barking, tongue-in-mouth. Now what? Knowing that our impressions of Rex are close enough to the stored dog-idea to merit inclusion, but those of Felix aren't, involves knowing *how to use* that stored dog-image. Just having it isn't enough. This shows that Hume's minimal view of the contents and actions of the mind isn't sufficient to account for concepts either.

Berkeley and Hume both insist on a passive mind, storing nothing but dim mental photographs of particular experiences. But they nevertheless need to include some mental activity beyond merely dragging out the photograph album: Berkeley's mind needs to classify many of these as similar, and needs somehow to associate them with each other; Hume's mind needs to know what features of the particular one to compare to the present case, and which to ignore. Both require a mind that can judge *similarity*, perhaps even as an innate capacity. Maybe we're better off with Locke. Or maybe some concepts are really innate. Why in the first place believe that there are no sorting-principles built into our brains?

Empiricists on God

Descartes believed the concept of God was innate, and Locke responded that if any concept were innate, that one would be: it's shared by all humanity, but God is not something we can sense. But he insisted that the concept was not innate; it was, instead, a complex idea composed of simple ideas derived from sense-experience. The idea of God is a combination of the ideas of superiority, infinity, power, wisdom, invisibility. Of course, we don't sense *infinity*, supposed to be involved in the concept of God, but empiricists characteristically try to account for this concept by saying that the concept of finitude is certainly given by experience, when we see the limits of earthly things, and it's an easy logical step from there to create an idea of non-finitude. (The same trick can be applied to the concept of invisibility.)

Locke uses the empiricist strategy outlined above for dealing with the concept of God: he tries to explain it in terms of sense-experience. But the second strategy, denying that it's a concept at all, is chosen by Hobbes. He asserts that we can't 'imagine' God. (To 'imagine' something, in his terms, is to form a mental image of it: what the empiricists took to be having a concept.) He says:

Whatever we imagine is finite. Therefore there is no idea or conception of anything we call infinite. No man can have in his mind an image of infinite magnitude, nor conceive infinite swiftness, infinite time, or infinite force, or infinite power ... And therefore the name of God is used, not to make us conceive him (for he is incomprehensible, and his greatness and power are inconceivable), but that we may honour him.

Hume appears to waver between these two, stating at one point:

The idea of God, as meaning an infinitely intelligent, wise, and good Being, arises from reflecting on the operations of our own mind, and augmenting, without limit, those qualities of goodness and wisdom.

but at another:

[Y]et I assert [God] is not the natural Object of any Passion or Affection, He is no Object either of the Senses or Imagination, & very little of the Understanding, without which it is impossible to excite any Affection.

Contemporary empiricists have sometimes argued that the idea of God, disconnected as it is from any possible sense-experience, must have no content at all – that 'God' is a word without meaning.

Empiricists on judgment

We have been looking at the first sort of application of the slogan 'Nothing in the intellect not previously in the senses': to concepts, 'ideas' in the terms of the empiricists. The second application is to what they called **judgments** – beliefs in propositions composed of these concepts. One has to have the concepts involved in order even to consider a proposition; thus, empiricists needed a theory of the origins of concepts. But having all the required concepts (*Rover, chasing*, and *Felix*) in mind does not amount to forming a judgment (believing that Rover is chasing Felix). One needs in addition to combine those concepts into a judgment, and to believe it.

For Hume, one makes a judgment – comes to or maintains a belief – when one combines ideas. As we've seen, there are, according to Hume, two kinds of judgment: belief in **relations of ideas** – analytic propositions – and belief in **matters of fact** – synthetic propositions. Analytic truths can be known a priori (by reasoning alone, because their denials were 'self-contradictions'), but synthetic truths can only be known a posteriori. Simple matters of fact (for example, 'Rover is barking') involving particulars can be known by direct observation. Sense-perception, then, is the origin, for empiricists, of all our important beliefs, and perception was invariably one of their chief concerns. We'll now turn to an examination of various philosophical theories and problems on perception.

Naïve realism and the argument from illusion

Our senses are in direct contact with the external world, and we see (hear, smell, feel, taste) things as they are, most of the time anyway. That's obvious, so of course you'll find philosophers trying to convince you that it's wrong. For much of the history of philosophy, in fact, many (or at times most) philosophers have thought it's wrong. They've come to call this obvious view **naïve realism** – *naïve* because it's a simple and unsophisticated view, held by those of us untutored in the subject, but corrected by sophisticated intellectual philosophy; *realism* because it holds that the direct and immediate objects of our perception have external reality.

Why deny that our senses put us in direct contact with the outside world? The main argument here is called the argument from illusion. Illusions are sense-experiences in which the outside world appears to us other than as it is. The example that seems to have appeared in almost every philosophical work on this subject for decades is that when you look at a straight stick half-immersed in water, it appears to be bent at the point where it emerges into the air. Another example with a long history is this: put one hand in a bucket of hot water for a while. Then quickly empty the bucket, fill it with roughly room-temperature water, and stick both hands in. The water will feel cold to the hand that was previously in hot water, and lukewarm to the other hand. Never mind which hand is feeling the water temperature the way it is: at least one of them must be wrong. Here's another famous one:

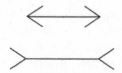

In this picture, the horizontal line in the top figure looks a lot smaller than the horizontal line in the bottom figure. But if you measure them, you'll find out that they're the same length.

These are all illusions, in which something appears to have a characteristic it doesn't really have.

Some other examples associated with the argument are, strictly speaking, not illusions but hallucinations, such as when you see pink snakes after having much too much to drink, or when Macbeth sees a dagger before him. These are cases in which something appears to be there which isn't. There's no significant difference in the argument if illusions or hallucinations are used as examples, so we'll mostly just concentrate on illusions.

Here's the argument, then:

1   When you're seeing an illusion, you're aware of something's having a characteristic which the real physical object out there, which you're supposedly perceiving, does not have.

2   So when you're seeing an illusion, what you're aware of is not that real physical object out there. It's something else. Call this something-else a **sense-datum**. (This simply means *what's given in sensation*. The plural of the term is 'sense-data').

3   But as far as your experience goes, there's no difference between how it seems when you're seeing an illusion and when you're perceiving in the ordinary way – in normal, non-illusory perception.

4   So in normal non-illusory perception, you're also aware of a sense-datum.

You probably need some explanation – and some convincing – regarding some of these steps in the argument.

Consider the bent stick. Step 1 urges you to accept that you're *aware of something bent*. But the stick out there in front of you is not bent. Objection: what I'm aware of is that stick, and that stick is not bent, so I'm *not* aware of something bent: I'm aware of something *not bent*. Reply: you know it's not really bent, but forget about this: what we're talking about is your *immediate awareness*. You might figure out that the stick is really straight, but we're not talking about an *inference* from your awareness, but about the character of that awareness itself.

Step 3 and the inference to Step 4 also call for some justification. Compare what happens when you look at a straight stick not immersed in water. Here too you're directly aware of something. The difference here is that what's out there (you think) matches your awareness – they're both straight. But as far as your experiences are concerned, there's absolutely no difference between the cases in which you see a bent stick 'as it is' and in which you see a straight stick as bent – 'as it isn't'. There's no way to distinguish from the inside – from the character of your experience – between perception that's 'normal' and that's illusory. So in 'normal' – that is, non-illusory – perception, you're also not directly aware of external objects; what you're directly aware of is, similarly to the first case, an internal appearance, a **sense-datum**.

More arguments for sense-data

Here is a simpler argument for the existence of sense-data. Imagine that Cameron and Andrew are both looking at an apple. They're in different perceptual states. Even though those perceptual states are very much like each other, they're not exactly alike; but even if they were exactly alike, the perceptual states they're in are *separate entities*: Cameron is in his particular perceptual state, not Andrew's, and Andrew is in his. That means that Cameron is aware of one thing, and Andrew is aware of a different thing. Call those things sense-data.

Here's a further argument. The light from the nearest-known star takes over four years to get here, and others are much further away. So when you look at the night sky, you're not seeing any stars or galaxies as they are when you look at them. Some of them may even have stopped existing during the time it takes for their light to get to you. So what you're seeing – the object of your perception – can't be any of those stars or galaxies, because none of them is present to you at the moment of perception. All earthly objects are much closer, of course, so the time-lag is much shorter; but there's some time-lag for anything you sense. So in all cases there's only indirect perception. What's directly perceived must be present at the moment of perception: and only sense-data fill that requirement.

Problems with sense-data

Sense-data are unusual items. It seems that they always are as they appear. (If they sometimes appeared otherwise than they are, then they would be subject to the argument from illusion!) But there's a problem here, arising from the fact that they are essentially *private*. Only you can experience your sense-data – nobody else can. But if there's no public check on whether your beliefs about them are right or wrong, then the distinction between *being right* and *merely seeming to be right* disappears; and some philosophers take this to show not that one is always right about one's sense-data, but rather that it doesn't make any sense to talk about being right about them at all.

Here are other peculiarities about sense-data:

They don't exist unperceived.

They're supposed to be mental entities, but they also, it seems, have physical properties. When something looks green to you, for example, then the sense-datum you have *is* green; but it's weird, maybe meaningless, to ascribe a colour to a mental item. (Only physical things have colours.)

When something turns from light green to dark green, are there two sense-data here, one replacing the other, or just one changing one?

The problem of the speckled hen. Suppose you're looking at a hen which has exactly forty-seven speckles on the side facing you. You then have a sense-datum which is hen-shaped and speckled, but how many speckles are there on the sense-datum? You haven't counted, and it doesn't seem to you that there are exactly forty-seven speckles, but neither does it seem to you that there are more or less than forty-seven speckles. Sense-data are as they seem, so the sense-datum does not have more or less than forty-seven speckles, nor does it have exactly forty-seven speckles. It has, we'd have to say, an indeterminate number of speckles – surely more than ten and less than 200, but no particular number in-between.

The strangeness of the idea of sense-data motivates a re-examination of the arguments that introduced this idea. Critics have often objected to Step 2. Here the argument urges us to accept the fact that (for example) the stick looks bent implies that there is something bent we see. But nothing is bent. Something *seems* bent, and that's the stick we see.

A way of understanding what's supposed to be the problem with sense-data theory is to apply the internalism/externalism distinction we looked at earlier. In an externalist understanding of what's going on when S sees O, there exists an external object O, and S is in a perceptual relation with that object. So we can infer from the fact that S sees O that O exists. This sort of relation has sometimes been called an **action–object relation**. Another example of this sort of relation is *S kicks O*. In both cases, O is the external object to which that action is directed. But contrast this with an internalist understanding of what's going on when S sees O. Internalism understands what's involved in something to do with S as a matter exclusively of S's internal states. Thus when you see a bent stick or a dagger, this is entirely a matter of your internal states – your visual and perhaps cognitive experience. What's going on understood this way is that you're having a bent-stick-seeing-experience, or a dagger-seeing-experience, and it's irrelevant whether or not there really is a bent stick or a dagger out there. You can see a bent stick or a dagger (understood this way) even when there's no bent stick or dagger there.

Both ways of talking and thinking about perception seem to be acceptable and to have a point. When Macbeth tells his psychiatrist that he saw a dagger the other day, should the psychiatrist, knowing that this is just another one of his hallucinations, take what he said as true? Well, yes and no. Yes, if he understands what Macbeth says in internalist terms: Macbeth really does have dagger-seeing experiences. No, if he understands what Macbeth says in externalist terms: there wasn't any dagger out there to be seen. It looks like there's an ambiguity in the verb *to see*: it might be meant, or understood, in either externalist or internalist terms. We'll mark the difference by a subscript: seeing$_e$ and seeing$_i$, respectively.

Now we have a way to explain exactly what apparently went wrong in the argument. We start out imagining (for example) that S is aware of – sees – something bent, but this is true only if 'sees' = 'sees$_i$' because what's clearly meant here is that S is having a bent-thing-seeing-experience, in the absence of anything bent. But then we're to conclude from this that there's something bent that S is seeing, but this conclusion is valid only if 'sees' = 'sees$_e$' because only in the externalist sense does it follow that what S is said to see really exists. This argument, then, analyzed this way, appears to be a clear case of fallacious reasoning, of the sort called *equivocation*: using a term with two different meanings at different stages of the argument, slipping from one meaning to the other. Step 1 uses an internalist sense of awareness, to convince us that S is aware of something bent. But in Step 2, the implication is drawn that what one is aware of exists; so Step 2 relies on an externalist sense of awareness.

The adverbial theory

In the stick-in-water illusion, a straight stick is seen *as bent* – that is, it's seen in a certain way. Because this is seeing$_i$, then a better way to think of it than in action-object terms, telling what the object that's seen is like, would be to describe what kind of visual experiencing it is. Grammatically speaking, we describe an act, telling what kind of act it is, or in what way it's done, using an adverb. Thus the **adverbial theory of perception**: in the case of seeing$_i$ a bent stick, we can describe this case as seeing the (straight) stick *bent-ly* – not a real word, but a made-up adverb meaning *in a bent manner*. (Similarly, when Macbeth sees his dagger, he's not seeing$_e$ anything; he's simply seeing *dagger-ly*.) Thus the adverbial theory explains what's happening when we see$_i$ a bent stick without postulating a weird object of perception.

Those impressed by the sense-data theory will object that this adverbial business doesn't do justice to our real experience. Imagine, for example, hallucinating a dagger. There really is an *object* of your experience, something you're seeing$_e$, isn't there?

But those who don't accept an action-object analysis of illusion and hallucination still sometimes find this adverbial theory insufficient. What is this bent-ly anyway? The word is made up, and it needs some explanation. But the adverbial theory, at least as far as we've taken it, gives no explanation.

Here's a candidate for explaining adverbial descriptions of visual experiences: seeing x-ly is the sort of experience one gets from seeing$_e$ something that is in fact x, *under normal conditions*. Under abnormal conditions, seeing$_e$ something that is in fact x can result in seeing which is not x-ly. When you see$_e$ a straight stick under normal conditions, it looks straight – that is (according to the adverbial theory) you are seeing something straight-ly. But under certain abnormal conditions, for example, when the stick is half-immersed in water, it looks bent. Under normal conditions, when you stick your hand in a bucket of warm water, it feels warm – in the adverbial-theory-language, you sense (feel?) warm-ly. But under some abnormal conditions, for example, when that hand has just been in a bucket of hot water, that warm water will feel cool-ly.

There are two problems with this view. First, even though the idea of 'normal conditions' seems to make some intuitive sense – we can see the point – nevertheless what's needed here, some philosophers argue, is a principled way of explaining what normal conditions really are. Of course, usually when we see$_i$ a bent stick we also see$_e$ a bent stick. But what perception conditions count as 'normal' doesn't seem to be a matter of frequency, because the most common conditions for perceiving something are sometimes not the 'normal' ones. It's sometimes said that a circular coin seems oval when seen from any position not at right angles from the plane of the coin – but coins are very rarely seen at right angles. What are 'normal conditions' for seeing colours? They can seem quite different when seen in sunlight when the sun is high in the sky, or in sunlight close to dawn or sunset, or in incandescent lighting, or in fluorescent lighting.

But here's another problem. On the classical view, we perform some sort of inference, if only unconscious, from the internal way things seem to the way we believe they are. But on the 'normal conditions' view, the only way we have to describe the way things seem is on the basis of how they are – that is, *something seems x-ly to S* means that S is having the experience that would be had if experiencing something that's really x under normal conditions. So our judgments about how something seems depend on the way things are; but classical empiricists also want to insist that our judgments about the way things are depend on the way things seem. Can we have things both ways?

A deeper objection – one we'll come back to – about the idea of sense-data is that they seem to shield us from reality – unnecessarily. This problem arises, in one way or another, in the internalist views we've looked at earlier. For example, if we make justification a matter of what's going on inside one's mind, then how are we ever to connect it to the likelihood of producing true belief – belief corresponding to the external world? In the case of present concern, the internalist view of perception, as strictly internal experience, raises the prospect of a similar impossibility of getting outside one's head. If all we directly experience is sense-data, what ever makes us think that we know anything at all about the external reality they're supposed *sometimes* to represent?

It appears, then, that we're in for an insoluble problem: how to establish that our perceptual experience corresponds to the actual world. Philosophical sceptics ask philosophers to prove that it does. Can this be accomplished?

In the next chapter, we'll look at this sceptical problem, and others that empiricists get themselves into.

8

Scepticism

Scepticism is the philosophical outlook which doubts what others take to be true, or which argues that what others take to be knowledge isn't that at all. It has a long and distinguished history in philosophy. We find sceptics in the Western philosophical tradition since before Socrates – wherever there is philosophy, there is scepticism.

When philosophers raise sceptical questions about the meaningfulness of widely accepted concepts, or about the truth of what's generally believed, their motivation is sometimes constructive – they intend to provide a better account of a concept, or a justification for a belief which didn't have a good one. What we've seen earlier in Descartes' writing is a good example of this sort of scepticism. In his *Meditations* he begins by giving reasons to doubt all our beliefs, but very soon begins the reconstruction process, to restore certainty for those for which this is possible, and to give some sort of practical reasonability to the rest. We end up more or less where we started, but with what Descartes claims is a firm foundation.

Often, however, sceptics don't have something better to propose: sometimes, in fact, they argue that there can't be a good account of some concept, or a good justification for a belief. Sometimes when this is the case, the sceptic advises us simply to dispose of that concept or belief. Hume probably thought that the concept of God should thus be jettisoned. In his second quotation, in Chapter 7 above, he does not go so far as to draw this conclusion – expressing atheist views was dangerous in his day; but since he clearly argues elsewhere that any supposed idea that does not come from experience is nonsense, and should be dropped, some Hume scholars argue that this is what he must have been thinking.

On the other hand, often such disposal would be impossible, or might amount to madness. We've already had a glance at scepticism about the belief in the existence of the external world – many philosophers have wondered how this might be justified, and have criticized attempts to do so; some have even concluded that it is impossible. But none has urged us to give up that belief. We couldn't if we tried. Only insane people succeed.

A third general approach taken by sceptics lies somewhere between the constructive approach, which intends to supply an adequate account that was missing, and the destructive approach, which denies that any such account may be given. It attempts to provide an explanation of the concept, or a justification for the belief, but one that reinterprets things significantly. Critics of this sort of **sceptical solution** reply that what it offers does not explain what they meant by that concept, that it changes the subject – talking about a different belief altogether. We'll see some instances of what could be taken as this approach in a moment.

Towards the end of this chapter, we'll talk about the most far-reaching and most basic sceptical problem in epistemology – the problem of the existence of the external world. Before we get there, however, we'll examine how empiricists raise sceptical doubts about our beliefs about causation, and about the justification of any general belief.

Empiricists on cause

Kant, as we've seen earlier, argues that the idea of cause, and the principle that everything has a cause, are non-empirical presuppositions of all experience; but how can an empiricist account for this idea and principle? Consider what you actually see when you think that one event is causing another: for example, you see one billiard ball moving to touch a second, followed by the second moving away. What you don't see is the first *causing* the second to move. Empiricists, then, are faced with these questions: where do we get the idea of causation? How can experience ever justify a belief that one event causes another?

Locke claims that causation is an 'idea of reflection' which derives from introspection of the operations of our own minds, in which, he thinks, we can directly experience causation. Hume finds no such introspective idea, and worries at length about where our idea of causal connections might come from. It's a very important matter, he thinks, since 'by means of that relation alone we can go beyond the evidence of our memory and senses'. Without it, the world is just one event and another; cause-and-effect relations between these events provide a structure.

Hume agreed with the critics of empiricism that we do not observe anything like an external 'causal power'. All we observe when we say that X causes Y is that Y follows X. What leads us to claim that X causes Y is, he claims, merely that we've observed the constant conjunction of Xs and Ys: they always, or usually, occur together, X before Y, and contiguous in space. 'After a repetition of similar instances, the mind is carried by habit, upon the appearance of one event, to expect its usual attendant, and to believe that it will exist.' This habit in us, not the external facts, is what leads us to say that X has the causal power to produce Y, that X determines Y.

Hume thus gives us a sceptical solution to the problem of causation. His account leaves out what many other philosophers have taken for granted: that the causal relation is a genuinely objective feature of reality, one we can discover.

As you can imagine, this account of our concept of causation has produced a good deal of disbelief in Hume's critics, many of whom think that this is not really an account of the concept of cause in terms of our sense-experiences; rather, it's a refusal (implausible to many) to allow that we have any such concept. Hume certainly does deny that we have anything like a full-fledged idea of causation, involving the power of one event to bring about another. What he will allow us is a radically minimalist idea, one that many philosophers have found unsatisfactory.

The problem of induction

Hume treats our expectation that Ys will continue to follow Xs as a mere habit of mind, caused by past experience of Ys following Xs. But, we might ask, doesn't the fact that Ys followed Xs in the past *justify* our expectation that things will continue to act that way? Even if we accept his deflationary account of the causal relation as amounting to nothing more than regular association together, still, don't we have real knowledge of the future, given our past experience?

Hume answers:

> As to past experience, it can be allowed to give direct and certain information of those precise objects only, and that precise period of time, which fell under its cognisance; but why this experience should be extended to future times, and to other objects, which for aught we know, may be only in appearance similar – this is the main question on which I would insist. The bread, which I formerly ate, nourished me … but does it follow, that other bread must also nourish me at another time. … The consequence seems nowise necessary.

This is Hume's famous **problem of induction**. Induction here is thought of as the process of reasoning that because something has held in the past, that it's probable that it will hold in the future; or, more generally, that since an observed part of a class

of things has a certain characteristic, the rest of that class probably does too. We can think of this process as summed up by the
Principle of Induction: that (roughly speaking) the characteristics of observed instances will hold of unobserved instances.
Induction has much wider application than judgments about
causes. Every generalization – every belief about *general kinds*
of things, as opposed to beliefs about particular individual items
– depends on induction for justification. But what justifies
induction?

Hume argued that this Principle could not be justified. He
recognized three possible sources for justification:

A proposition about a particular individual case is justified by
    individual observation.
A general analytic proposition is justified merely by thought (a
    priori).
A general synthetic proposition is justified by induction from
    several past observations.

Now consider our justification of the Principle of Induction. It's
a general proposition, not a particular one, so it can't be justified
by an individual observation. It's clearly not analytic – its denial
is not a 'self-contradiction'. But can it be established by reasoning from past instances? Let's try:

> In the past, by and large, it has been observed that use of induc-
> tive reasoning has been successful in prediction; so we can
> conclude that it's probably a reliable method to use in new
> cases.

But this attempt to establish the validity of the Principle uses
induction to justify induction. It's circular reasoning: it assumes
exactly what it's trying to prove. That sort of reasoning is
obviously illegitimate.

Hume concludes that there can be no rational justification
for induction. This is a shockingly sceptical conclusion:

induction, Hume thinks, is the basis of *all* our important general knowledge. (Analytic generalizations, as we've seen, are unimportant.) Of course Hume does not urge that we abandon this method of providing justification for our beliefs in general propositions even though it itself is unjustifiable. We couldn't if we wanted to: it appears to him to be an unbreakable habit of mind, what we would call hard-wired into our brains – a matter of instinct shared by all the other higher animals. But he does not think this fact provides *justification* for this method.

The problem of induction is just the sort of thing Kant's approach is designed to deal with. He'd agree with Hume that the Principle of Induction is synthetic, and that it can't be established by observation. He would claim, however, that this is one of several presuppositions that are necessary for rational experience of the world, so reflection on this fact can provide a priori justification for it.

Some philosophers have found the Kantian response plausible. Hume would agree, in fact, that inductive reasoning is an extremely important and basic part of rationality. But is Kant correct that presupposing the Principle of Induction is the only possible way one can rationally approach one's world? Let's try to imagine two organisms very different from humans who don't approach the world that way. They'll have to be aliens from another planet: Hume's probably right that even animals on earth use induction. Consider, then:

Mork from Mars, who reasons from past experience by using *counter-induction*: having observed that all or the large majority of Martian hairy worms can fly, he concludes that the next Martian hairy worm he sees *won't* be able to fly.

Mindy from Venus, who doesn't reason on the basis of past experience at all: having observed that all or the large majority of Venusian pickle-trees drop their fruit in the autumn, she comes to no conclusion at all about when the next Venusian pickle-tree she sees will drop its fruit. She predicts things by flipping a coin.

We can at least *conceive* of these alternatives to induction; does this show that Kant was wrong?

Imagine trying to convince Mork and Mindy that they're making mistakes. You might point out to Mork that the method he uses has been a dismal failure in the past; but, for him, this just counts as evidence that it will work the next time. You might point out to Mindy that the method she uses has not worked very well in the past, that her predictions would have been much more successful if she had predicted continuations of the previously observed patterns. But she'd be unperturbed by her past failures; she take them as irrelevant. Note here that these two alternatives to induction 'justify' themselves circularly the same way induction itself does!

Kant did not say that we couldn't imagine anyone reasoning in a way that didn't presuppose his a priori synthetic truths. What he said is that we couldn't imagine anyone reasoning *rationally* without presupposing them. Are Mork or Mindy then irrational? If calling them irrational is simply a way of saying that they're not doing the right kind of reasoning, then this might just be an expression of our prejudice in favour of our own thought processes, not a demonstration that there's something wrong with the way they're reasoning.

Some philosophers have thought that an appeal to the very idea of rationality was relevant here. Using one's past experience as a guide to the future is, after all, *exactly what we mean* by 'rationality'. Other philosophers, however, have not found this approach helpful; it seems that you can't show that a method of arriving at beliefs is the proper one just by appealing to a definition. If that's what 'rationality' means, then we can ask a new question: why does rationality justify beliefs?

Another approach to Hume's problem has been to object to the terms in which it's stated. Look, these objectors say in effect, the only way some practice can be vindicated is by showing that it's worked well in the past. But this sort of vindication is not possible in Hume's case, so it's not surprising that there's no defence for induction! It's like asking somebody to look at something while keeping their eyes closed, or to sing a song without making a sound. It's asking for the impossible. Any request to do the impossible is an illegitimate nonsense request, and nobody should be expected to try to respond to it.

This reply, however, has not always been found satisfactory. Hume, of course, realizes – in fact, *argues* – that there's no way induction can be justified, because of the circularity in this case of inductive justification. He agrees that asking for justification is asking the impossible. That's just his point! This reply then appears not to solve Hume's problem, but rather just to repeat it.

The problem of the existence of the external world

This problem is like the ones we've just been looking at. Here again we're being asked for the justification for a kind of inference; in this case, it's an inference from the way things seem to the way they (often) are. This problem, sometimes called **the problem of the existence of the external world**, has perplexed epistemology throughout its history. If we must infer the way things are from the way things seem, what could ever justify this inference?

The way things are is never logically entailed by the way they seem. It does not follow deductively from the fact that something seems red to you – that you have a red sense-datum – that there's something red out there.

Is it an inductive, probabilistic inference? That when something seems red to you, and when it also seems that there's nothing abnormal in the conditions of observation, then *probably* there's something red out there? That looks like a perfectly reasonable inference, but is it really justified? In order to justify a non-deductive (probabilistic) inference from X to Y, one needs to have had experience of X's being accompanied by Y in some way – grounds for linking X and Y. (Never mind the problem of induction.) Dark clouds and a falling barometer justify the inference that it will rain because of all our experience linking rain with those phenomena. But if we never directly experience the external world – if the only way available for knowing about it is by inference from the way things seem, from our inner experience – then we *never* have any ground for linking anything in our experience with anything outside. It seems, then, that we never have any justification for the **Realist Hypothesis** – the view that there is a real physical world out there that we're perceiving.

It's this line of reasoning, more than any other in the entire study of philosophy, that gives the discipline a bad name.

Alternatives to the Realist Hypothesis

Before we look at responses to this problem, you should know about some picturesque versions of essentially the same argument.

Following are three alternatives to the Realist Hypothesis. We'll call them **Unrealist Hypotheses**. In each case, we wonder why the Realist Hypothesis is to be preferred.

1 **The Evil Demon Hypothesis**. Consider this hypothesis: an evil demon, able to control your thoughts, has been giving you hallucinations; as a result, your sense-experience

never provides any basis for belief about what the outside world is like. Unless you can show why this hypothesis should be rejected, then your beliefs about the external world are unjustified.

2   **The I-Might-Be-Dreaming Hypothesis**. You're dreaming right now. A dream seems, to a dreamer, just like ordinary perception seems to a person who is awake; we take dream experience to be nothing but hallucination. If you're dreaming right now, reality is nothing like the way you're experiencing it. Can you show that this is not the case? (Some philosophers report having dreams in which they ask themselves whether they are then dreaming, and come to the confident conclusion that they are not.)

3   **The Brain-in-a-Vat Hypothesis**. At birth, your brain was removed from your body, and kept alive by immersion in a vat full of nutritive solution. The input and output channels of your brain are connected to a giant computer which analyses your brain's output, and feeds in what you take to be sensory input. You are nothing but a brain-in-a-vat. Accordingly, all your sense-experience is hallucination, and it never provides any basis for belief about what the outside world is like. Unless you can show why the hypothesis that you're a brain-in-a-vat (which we'll abbreviate as **BIV**) should be rejected, then your beliefs about the external world are unjustified.

The Evil Demon and I-Might-Be-Dreaming Hypotheses were both invented by Descartes. The Brain-in-a-Vat Hypothesis was created by the contemporary American philosopher Hilary Putnam; a similar idea may be familiar to you from the film *The Matrix*.

Attempts to defeat the Unrealist Hypotheses

Here are some philosophical responses to this argument, followed by responses to the responses. See if you think if any of them are any good.

Common Sense. 'Everybody knows that there is an external world, and that it's by and large the way it seems to us. Here is my right hand. Everyone knows that their own right hand exists (and a whole lot of other things too). That's only common sense.'

That reply doesn't seem adequate to most philosophers. Insisting that a hypothesis conflicts with common sense isn't regarded, in general, as a good argument against it. There have been many beliefs that were considered obviously true, just common sense, but which were false, or at least unjustified. Note here that the truth of these hypotheses is not at issue. Nobody who is sane could be convinced of any of them. What is being asked for here is reason to believe they're false – justification of the belief that they are false. Pointing out what's just common sense doesn't provide this.

Comparative believability. 'No argument could ever convince me that there's any reason at all to doubt my belief that my right hand is here now. That belief is so strong that I would always, instead, doubt the soundness of any argument that questioned it.'

Sane people would always prefer the Realist Hypothesis to any of the three Unrealist Hypotheses. Similarly, they would always prefer to doubt any reason to believe one of these three, rather than to accept it. The belief in the Realist Hypothesis in preference to all of these is thus probably unshakable – perhaps what we called in an earlier chapter *indubitable* or *incorrigible*. But this does not make it infallible; more importantly, this psychological fact about the belief gives no reason at all to think it's true – no justification.

Testability. 'If you're unsure about the existence of any particular thing in the external world – thinking maybe your experience is just a hallucination – there are ways of finding out. If you think you're just hallucinating a strawberry, you can try to touch it, smell it, taste it. If you're successful at all this, then that shows there really is a strawberry there.'

But this sort of test does not rule out any of the Unrealist Hypotheses. The evil demon, or the dream, or the giant computer could just as well produce the feeling, taste, and smell of the strawberry in your mind.

Testimony of others. 'Another way to make sure is to ask other people.'

Again, the fact that you experience the agreement of others doesn't show that any of the three Unrealist Hypotheses is false. Others may be hallucinating what you do; or you may be hallucinating their agreement (or their existence).

The best explanation. 'The Realist Hypothesis is the best theory to explain our experience.'

This argument is more worthy of serious examination than the others. In science, we sometimes establish the existence of things that aren't observed – even sometimes *can't* be observed – as the best explanation for what is observed. Nobody has ever seen an electron, and, given their tiny size and their resultant inability to reflect light, nobody could ever see one. But their existence is the best explanation for all sorts of things that are observed. Similarly, it is argued, the best explanation for our experience is the Realist Hypothesis.

The idea that we're justified in going beyond what's experienced by the senses represents a significant departure from traditional empiricism. When the account of theory including postulation of unobservables was proposed by philosophers of science early in the twentieth century, there was considerable resistance from empiricists still strongly in the Humean tradition, who preferred to think of science as generalization (by

induction) from observation. By now, however, most philosophers find unobservables acceptable.

However, it's necessary to ask, in the current case: what is
supposed to make the Realist Hypothesis the best explanation of
our experience? Compare the Unrealist Hypotheses. Any of
these, it appears, could explain everything we experience as
well. Why choose the Realist Hypothesis over any of these?

It's sometimes replied that even though each of the Unrealist
Hypotheses might account for all our experiences, the Realist
Hypothesis does this *better*. One widely accepted criterion for a
good explanation is simplicity: the hypothesis which involves
the least complexity, the fewest number of unexplained or ad
hoc assumptions and conceptual contortions, is the one to
accept. (This test is called **Ockham's Razor**.) So, for example,
it's argued that the simplest explanation for the fact that strawberry-looks are usually accompanied by strawberry-smells and
strawberry-tastes is that there really are strawberries which look,
smell, and taste like that. On any Unrealist Hypothesis, we'd
have to make additional unwarranted assumptions: that the
demon or the brain scientist just wanted these experiences to go
together, for some unexplained reason; or that these regularities
were often represented together in your dreams – though
nobody could know why.

William of Ockham (English, c. 1287–1347) was among the greatest
of the medieval philosophers. His principle, that one should not
claim the existence of more entities than are theoretically necessary
(or more generally, and somewhat historically inaccurately, that the
simplest explanation is best) has become known as Ockham's Razor
because it advises cutting away what's unnecessary. (It might have
more accurately been called 'Ockham's eraser' – in his day, razors
were used to erase unwanted matter from the animal-skin parch-
ment used for writing.)

But is the Realist Hypothesis really simpler? The explanation for our experience given the Realist Hypothesis consists in the whole enormous complex of everyday and scientific theory about the external world. This is hardly simple! Compare how the three Unrealist Hypotheses explain experience: just by the whim of the evil demon or the programming of the giant computer, or by the random 'logic' of dreams. Of course, none of these tells us why any particular part of our experience is the way it is, rather than some other way; but in each case, this is something we probably could never understand. What we need here is a better understanding of exactly what simplicity amounts to. But even if, on some clear understanding of what simplicity is, the Realist Hypothesis really is simplest of the four, we want to know why the simplest hypothesis among alternatives is most likely to be true. Is it because the universe really is basically simple? That sounds unlikely; and how could we justify *that* claim?

Contextualism. What's necessary for S's belief to count as knowledge claims depends on the context. (This is what is sometimes called the **contextualist** position.) So in ordinary contexts, your experience is completely sufficient evidence for knowledge that there's a cup of coffee on the desk in front of you, and for the rest of our ordinary realist beliefs. But in the context in which we consider the Unrealist Hypotheses, the standards required for knowing are greatly elevated, to the point at which they can't be met. So the contextualist grants that we can't justify the belief that any of them is false, but this doesn't matter, because it has no effect on our knowledge of everyday matters.

Note the peculiar result of this position. It grants that you don't know you're not a BIV. And, clearly, if you were a BIV, then you wouldn't *know* you have hands, because you wouldn't have any. But it insists that you *do* know that you have hands. This seems very odd. Compare a more usual case. Suppose Fred told you that he didn't dent your car. Suppose in addition, you don't know that 'Fred is a liar' is false. If Fred really is a liar, then you don't know that he didn't dent your car. So it follows that you don't know he didn't dent your car.

Externalism. Our words, and the thoughts they express, mean what they do because their use has a history of causal connection with the objects in the real world they refer to. If you were a BIV, you wouldn't have the appropriate causal historical connections with real brains or real vats that are required for the ability to say or think 'I might be a brain in a vat.' So either the supposition that you are a BIV is meaningful but false – because you aren't – or else you can't even make that supposition. Therefore the supposition is false.

But, some philosophers reply, the idea that in order to have a thought about Xs one must be connected in some way with real Xs is not plausible. Can't someone think about Santa Claus, despite never having causal interaction with Santa? Couldn't someone who had never interacted with a genuine external strawberry have strawberry-hallucinations and thereby think about strawberries?

An interesting thought-experiment to test these positions is the story of Swampman:

> Ed is walking through the swamp when a bolt of lightning strikes him and kills him. Simultaneously, another bolt strikes the swamp nearby, and rearranges a pile of swamp gunk, by coincidence, to resemble Ed exactly, molecule-by-molecule. Call the guy instantaneously created Swampman. Because his brain is completely identical with Ed's, he picks himself up, and returns to Ed's house, and resumes Ed's life. But when he asks Ed's wife, 'Where did I leave my keys?' is he actually referring to Ed's keys?

Some philosophers react to the story by saying that Swampman can't think or talk about Ed's keys, despite the fact that he makes those sounds, and appears satisfied when he finds them. The reason is that, lacking any history at all, he has not had a history of learning and using his language, and thinking his thoughts, connected to any external objects. So there's no way of interpreting what he means by his language, or what he's thinking about. There is no fact of the matter, really, about what Swampman means or thinks about. This is **externalism about meaning and thinking**.

But on the other hand, some philosophers object, the proper moral of the Swampman story is not that Swampman can't think about anything. It's rather that, lacking information about his causal history, we can't *interpret* him as meaning one thing rather than another. That doesn't mean that he doesn't mean something. And other philosophers insist that, because Swampman's brain is coincidentally a duplicate of the late Ed's brain, what Swampman means by what he says, and what he thinks about, is exactly what Ed would have thought about. When he asks Mrs Ed where those keys are, he means Ed's keys. Still other philosophers argue that, since he acts just as Ed would have, and his brain works just as Ed's would have, he thinks and means just what Ed would have meant.

But suppose that you accept the idea that, like Swampman, the BIV can't think about things, and therefore cannot entertain the hypothesis that it's a BIV, any more than it can think about anything in the external world. Does this help with the problem of the existence of the external world? If there weren't any external world, according to this approach, we couldn't think that there was an external world or that there wasn't; but does that show that there really is one? Our belief in the external world, according to this perspective, is either true or isn't really a belief in the external world at all. But this doesn't show its true.

Solipsism

A significant number of philosophers have taken the problem of the existence of the external world to be insoluble – and have accepted its conclusion that realism is unjustified. What then?

One alternative to realism is **solipsism**. That's the view that the only thing that exists is the contents of one's own mind. People who really believe this need psychiatric help. No philosopher has really believed this – at least, none who made his or her position known. (Why, after all, would a genuine solipsist attempt to communicate?) But philosophers certainly have argued that realism has no more justification than solipsism.

One argument against solipsism is the same externalist argument used above against the BIV Hypothesis. If solipsism were true, then the single mind (yours!) that existed in the universe couldn't say or believe anything. It couldn't, for example, believe that there's a strawberry-taste experience, or that there's no strawberry out there: lacking connections to real strawberries, all this talk and thought would have no meaning. You can't be a solipsist and consistently think or claim that you are – because you can't think or claim anything. But again, maybe this doesn't prove much.

Phenomenalism

Traditional empiricists hold that language and thought get their meaning and reference through connection with our *internal* experience. So when we think or talk about strawberries, for example, what we're really referring to is a collection of straw-berry-sense-experiences: strawberry-looks, strawberry-tastes, strawberry-smells, and so on. That collection can be the only thing strawberries are for us. So strawberries don't cause these experiences – they *are* these experiences. There's no need to solve the problem of inference from experiences – experiences are all there is. This is the position called **phenomenalism**.

Phenomenalists do not believe, however, that for a strawberry to exist is merely for someone to have strawberry-experiences. There are an indefinite number of strawberry-experiences we might have, depending on the conditions under which they're experienced. Strawberries look one way if observed under sunlight, and another way under blue light, and a third way under yellow light. They taste one way if eaten with cream, and another way if eaten just after vinegar salad-dressing. So phenomenalists say that what there is for a strawberry to exist is that, in addition to some strawberry-experiences people have had, there are indefinitely many potential sense-experiences – experiences someone *would have* had *if ...* if what? If that person had looked, tasted, smelled, under conditions A or B or C ... Now, just try to list what sorts of potential sense-experience would be involved with the existence of a given strawberry. You can't complete this list, because it is indefinitely long: what a strawberry would look like if you saw one on a planet circling around, and illuminated by, the red star Betelgeuse; what one would taste like if you had a rare taste-disorder preventing you from tasting any sourness; and on and on. So a central objection against phenomenalism is the impossibility of specifying what a strawberry or anything else is.

In addition, because items on this list each tell what sensation would be had under some particular conditions, the phenomenalist would owe us an explanation of what would constitute being under those conditions. (How could a phenomenalist explain what being on a planet circling around, and illuminated by, the red star Betelgeuse was?)

Nobody thinks that strawberries pop in and out of existence, depending on whether anyone's observing them or not. They still exist when unobserved. There are even strawberries that rot on the vine and are never observed through their whole existence. Are these constituted by wholly potential experiences, and no actual ones? Thinking of unobserved objects as consisting of nothing but merely possible experiences is very odd. One of the first of the great British empiricists, George Berkeley, tried to solve this problem by postulating that no experiences were experienced by nobody: all experiences that are merely possible for any human are actually being experienced – by God. (Berkeley was a bishop.)

In response to Berkeley's problem, the witty writer Msgr Ronald Knox wrote this famous limerick:

> There was once a man who said, 'God
> Must think it exceedingly odd
> If he finds that this tree
> Continues to be
> When there's no one about in the Quad.'

And here's the anonymous response to Knox's poem:

> Dear Sir, Your astonishment's odd:
> I am always about in the Quad.
> And that's why the tree
> Will continue to be,
> Since observed by, Yours faithfully, God.

Berkeley's solution to this problem has not been found satisfactory by many philosophers. The whole idea of a large bunch of actual but mostly possible sensations with objective existence has seemed to most a terribly strange idea. Relying on God's observation to explain how this can be is, perhaps, an instance of what we've already seen in Descartes: when all else fails, that's where you bring in God. This looks like philosophical cheating.

Does externalism help?

The problem of justifying belief in the existence of the external world has been considered, so far, mostly in the context of internalist epistemology. Would the problem go away for externalists? The quick answer is no, and here's why. Let's look, for example, at externalist ideas of perception. Externalists don't think of perception as having internal sense-data as its object: rather, what we perceive are features of the outside world. So if you see a mongoose, then on the externalist understanding, there is a mongoose there. Accordingly, the truth of *I see X*, for any X, implies the existence of an external X. Does this solve the problem? No. From the externalist perspective, we can now ask for justification of the belief that you're seeing a mongoose.

It's the old story of the wrinkle in the carpet. You push the wrinkle down in one place, and it pops up in another.

What's coming

The fact that the problem of the existence of the external world arises in the first place can be taken to show that something has gone wrong at a very basic level with the approaches philosophers have traditionally taken. In the next chapter, we'll look at several rather sweeping proposals for revision of the tradition.

9
New approaches to epistemology

During the last few decades a number of the assumptions previously made by epistemologists have been called into question, and some approaches to the subject have been proposed that are substantially different from the ones we have been looking at. In this final chapter, we'll have a look at some of these.

Naturalized epistemology

Descartes clearly and influentially reaffirmed what has been the standard a priori philosophical methodology assumed by most philosophers since then. He argued that the a posteriori empirical methods of science should have no place in epistemology, because epistemology was supposed to establish the proper subject matter and the grounds for validity of science. One can hardly do that by *using* science: that would be blatantly circular, assuming the validity of what we're trying to prove.

Later empiricist philosophers held that a priori methods can deal only with analytic matters. So they saw a sharp contrast between philosophy, which they supposed was a priori, thus composed of analytic truths and their consequences only, and science, which was a posteriori, composed of synthetic statements and generalizations from them. The job for philosophy, then, could only be the clarification of old concepts, the stipulation of new ones, and the exploration of the logical consequences of both. But some contemporary philosophers have held the revolutionary view that epistemology might have significant a posteriori empirical elements too – that it might be one of the empirical sciences.

Behind this position is what might be called a **naturalistic** outlook – the tendency to look at any phenomenon as *part of nature*, and to see science as the paradigm truth-seeking methodology – the best, in fact, the only, way to find out truth. Could epistemology be a science, like any other? Or could it at least require scientific input? We'll have a look at some different affirmative answers – views that advocate **naturalized epistemology**.

Externalist theories as naturalized

The externalist theories discussed earlier – the causal theory and reliabilism – are often thought of as substantially naturalized. The idea of a causally reliable indicator is a respectable category for natural science. Compare, for example, the way scientific observation has established that a rapidly falling barometer is a reliable indicator of a coming storm, or that the size of a white-blood-cell count indicates infection. Philosophers then might rely on the sciences (for example the psychology of perception) to tell us how we might have reliable indicators of the external world.

This scientific perspective assumes that one can tell reliable from unreliable processes – processes that give good information about the external world from those that don't – by experiment and observation: perception is quite reliable, because beliefs that are the immediate consequence of perception are almost always true; memory is reliable, but somewhat less so, since what one seems to remember usually happened, but sometimes didn't. Hunches are a much less reliable process. A psychologist interested in perception under different conditions will put subjects in the conditions being tested, and see what percentage of subjects' resulting beliefs are true; so of course the scientist must already know which beliefs are true and which not. Scepticism about the validity of these beliefs never comes up, nor should it; even less relevant in this context is general scepticism about the existence of the external world. Nevertheless, epistemologists can point out, with justice, that it does not follow from the fact that something is automatically assumed in everyday contexts or in science, that what is assumed is justified. In science and in everyday life, we haven't solved the basic problem of the existence of the external world – we've just ignored it. Maybe, of course, this problem is best dealt with that way!

Quine's naturalized epistemology

The naturalized epistemological approaches just considered are in some ways, however, traditionally a prioristic in their approach. Although they (in contrast to traditional epistemology) take scientific information to be relevant to epistemology, this information plays a subsidiary role to a priori philosophical considerations. They all ask the traditional philosophical questions – What counts as knowledge? What are we entitled to believe? – and try to answer them by using traditional a priori philosophical methods: weighing proposals against our intuitions, telling stories to test our reactions.

As we've seen, however, Quine rejects the distinctions between a priori and a posteriori knowledge, along with the distinction between analytic and synthetic sentences. According to Quine, we can't distinguish, within a theory, those parts that establish definitions (so are analytic) and those which are shown true or false by observation. So Quine clearly rejects Descartes' approach to epistemology, which treats it as a wholly a priori study, or the causal theories considered above, which distinguish between the a priori (traditionally philosophical) parts of the study, and the a posteriori (scientific) contributions.

For Quine, there is only one sort of knowledge, and that's scientific knowledge. Every theory is a scientific theory, and should be judged as such. That goes for epistemology too. Its aim is to understand the process in humans that leads from stimulation to belief. Thus epistemology is, for Quine, a branch of psychology – a study, as empirical as that of any science – of the ways we get knowledge.

Quine is explicit in advocating that we should avoid, rather than try to solve, the problem of the existence of the external world. It's impossible, Quine argues, to derive any propositions about the external world from the nature of internal experience. Like any science, epistemology, according to Quine, takes the external world for granted; once we see epistemology as a science, sceptical doubts about the external world evaporate. What we should think about instead – what we can successfully determine – is the process by which we really do form beliefs about the external world. Critics – traditional epistemologists – see Quine's views as proposing the abandonment of epistemology in favour of psychology.

Can naturalized epistemology be normative?

To call a theory **normative** is to say that it yields standards for what should and should not be done. As we've seen, traditional epistemology very often considers the standards for belief – whether, when, and why we're *entitled* to believe what we do. In a fairly widespread view, however, scientific theories are entirely descriptive: they tell you what happens and why it happens, not what *ought* to happen. Science, then, could be expected to tell us how people's psychology actually does work, not how it ought to. So the psychology of belief – what Quine proposes as a replacement for traditional epistemology – might be expected to tell us how people actually *do* come to their beliefs, not how they *should* – what leads people to believe, not whether they're justified.

At times, Quine seems to accept this consequence, and to insist that the proper study of knowledge should be merely descriptive. But there are passages in his work that suggest things are more complicated than this. In addition to the view that naturalistic epistemology is contained within psychology, Quine also holds that in a sense the rest of science is contained within epistemology. This is because epistemology, the science of knowledge, tells us what standards are in fact used in obtaining knowledge. Knowledge-getting is, after all, an activity which in fact does apply standards. Sometimes we judge that these standards are met – when a belief is reasonable, with proper backing – and sometimes we judge that it's not – a hunch, for example, or a guess. Quinean epistemology, then, discovers the standards we actually use for knowledge-getting. It doesn't *set* these standards, but it can tell us, in a way, that certain of our beliefs about the external world are justified, by revealing the standards we in fact apply to distinguish justified belief from unjustified. And, clearly, these standards are satisfied by most of our beliefs about externals. A Quinean epistemologist would ask: what else could you want from epistemology?

In reply, it's tempting to say that we do want more. Here's a story that might indicate where Quinean epistemology falls short of the normativity we might expect.

Dr Gzorpe is a native of the Doonga tribe, and he's also a Quinean epistemologist. Accordingly, he believes that part of his job is to discover the norms for legitimate belief formation that in fact operate. Now, in the Doonga tribe, information obtained from stimulation of the senses is deemed useful only for a small number of extremely practical day-to-day matters. For more important, more general matters, the Doonga rely on their dreams: a very vivid dream that p is taken to justify the belief that p. 'That's how general beliefs are justified', reports Gzorpe, 'by vivid dreams.'

We can agree that Gzorpe reports what the Doonga count as justification, but that doesn't appear to classical epistemologists to answer the question about what really is justification. (And, in this case, what the Doonga count as justification really isn't.) Compare, in this regard, the difference between two sorts of study people interested in ethics might pursue. They might ask, on one hand, what ethical standards are routinely used in their own culture, or in some other culture, to distinguish right from wrong. This is the study of *descriptive* ethics. Or they might ask what the real ethical standards are, the ones that distinguish genuine right from wrong. This is the study of *normative* ethics. Someone studying descriptive ethics would report that Nazis regard victimizing inferior races for the benefit of the Master Race as a good thing. But this doesn't imply that it really is a good thing. Traditionally, epistemology is supposed to be a normative study. Quine's epistemology appears simply to change the subject. It's anthropology, not epistemology.

Quine and circularity

Imagine this further twist: that when we ask Gzorpe how *he* knows that this is how they justify beliefs, he reports that he didn't do any empirical investigation – rather, he had a vivid dream that that's the way they do it. (He is, after all, a member of the tribe he's studying, and it's natural for him to use the standards of his group.) Gzorpe's epistemology both *reveals* the standards-governed methodology the Doonga use for knowledge, and *applies* that methodology and those standards. This story illustrates Quine's point that epistemology and the rest of the sciences are in a rather special position: each sets the rules for the other. Epistemology (as one of the sciences) is subject to all the standards and methods of any other science. But as the science of knowledge, it also sets the standards for all science. Quine is not bothered by this circularity. How else could a science study the standards of science other than by applying them?

Here's another circularity Quine cheerfully admits. You might recall Hume's problem of induction, and the argument that one cannot justify induction by relying on the past success of that reasoning process; to do so would be to assume just what's to be proved. But that's the way Quine wants to justify induction. When you ask for evidence about whether any method of truth-finding is likely to work, he argues, the right way (and the only way) to answer this question is the normal scientific way: by looking at how well it's worked in the past. In reply to the well-known objection about circularity, he agrees that this is circular; but, he adds, in effect, *so what?* The only way to answer any question is the scientific way. What else could you be looking for?

Evolution and the function of cognitive processes

Does that mean that naturalized epistemology can't deal with the evaluative questions that traditional epistemology has asked? Not necessarily. Let's look at some proposals.

First, consider the notion of *function*. This is an idea that shows up all over the place in the life sciences. The function of that floss surrounding milkweed seeds is to carry the seeds in the wind for wide distribution. The function of red blood cells is to transmit oxygen. The function of the insides of a hen's egg is to provide nourishment to the growing chick embryo. And so on. It appears that science can determine what the function of some biological feature or process is. And once function is determined, science can compare various sorts of feature or process which have that function, to see which accomplish it better or worse.

All along, we've been assuming that the function of belief-forming processes in humans is to produce *true* beliefs. If science can determine function, then this common-sense idea can be scientifically corroborated. Given this, then, science can determine how well various belief-forming processes in humans accomplish this task. (This, in fact, is exactly what some cognitive psychologists are doing right now.) Then science would tell us what beliefs are justified: those whose sources are processes that are good at performing their function.

But (and there's always a 'but' in philosophy!) is the function of our belief-forming processes really to get *true* belief? The fact that some feature or process has, in general, a particular result does not show that achieving that result is its function. Voltaire parodied this sort of reasoning in *Candide* when his philosopher explained that supporting eyeglasses is clearly the function of the nose. How do we decide when something has a certain function?

One proposal is to apply the idea of evolution here. If a feature or process evolved in organisms because those with that characteristic did better at staying alive and reproducing, then we can say that producing this advantage is the function of that characteristic. (Obviously noses did not evolve in humans to confer the advantages of eyeglass-support.) So we should ask: would the production of true beliefs confer biological advantage?

(Quine agrees that evolution is relevant here. In his treatment of induction, he argues that it's relevant that 'Creatures inveterately wrong in their inductions have a pathetic, but praiseworthy, tendency to die before reproducing their kind.')

You might guess that the more true beliefs an organism had, the better it would be at staying alive and reproducing. But this should not be assumed too quickly. Here are some reasons to doubt that this simple assumption is correct:

1   Given the finite capacities of memory and perceptual and other mental processes, it can't really be the case that the more true beliefs the better. At some point, more true beliefs would overload any system, and the organism would be worse off.

2   Sometimes survival is much better served by finite cognitive capacities if they're organized to produce a substantial proportion of false beliefs. For example, organisms can be better off programmed to think that any loud noise means danger, rather than to sort out the ones that really do indicate danger. That sorting-out would take time, and use up energy and capacity better directed elsewhere. This means that a process producing a higher percentage of false beliefs about the presence of danger might be better.

3   We can imagine that, in certain circumstances, false beliefs might themselves confer comparative biological advantage. For example, somebody who falsely overestimated his or her own abilities in some contexts might do much better than someone with an accurate assessment.

Epistemology as sociology

A quite different way of naturalizing epistemology shares Quine's idea that it's really a branch of science, but the science here is sociology, not psychology. This idea was given its initial impetus by an influential book, *The Structure of Scientific Revolutions*, published by Thomas Kuhn in 1962. Kuhn's topic is the social processes involved in scientific theory change.

Here is Kuhn's view of the dynamics of science. A theory is the dominant mode of thinking within a scientific community, providing its own vocabulary, conceptual schemes, methodology, and standards for acceptability. Newcomers are trained to think that way, and pushed to continue that mode of thought by social forces. The theory gives scientists (in Kuhn's influential word) *paradigms* regulating their thought and scientific activities. Within those paradigms, new findings can always be accommodated, leaving the framework intact, by making small changes; though these changes might not be entirely satisfactory. Eventually the strain imposed by these changes, of living with increasingly problematic old paradigms, builds up, and new paradigms appear. After a period of battle between scientists who hang on to the old and the advocates of the new, the latter may prove victorious, and in short order the old paradigms are abandoned for new ones. Kuhn's view, then, is that major change in science is not at all a matter of gradual adjustment to more factual evidence. It's much more like a social revolution.

To what extent this picture of the history of science is correct is a matter for debate among historians and sociologists of science. But it has been taken to have epistemological consequences. The most important one is this: Kuhn is taken to have shown that each scientific paradigm includes its own criteria for what counts as a justified belief, and for how seriously, if at all, contrary evidence is to be considered. And this holds not just for science, conceived narrowly as what professional scientists do, but for us in general, as knowers, with regard to the everyday things we believe. The cultural paradigms in our group for what counts as justified might be entirely different from those of another group. According to this view (which may not have been intended, exactly this way, by Kuhn, but which has been widely inferred from his ideas) there is no such thing as objective truth. There's only truth as recognized by the criteria for acceptable belief-formation, and the conceptual categories, of a particular society's paradigm; but that might not count as truth for another society, operating under a different paradigm. In one society, what's counted as truth is what results from empirical investigation, while another counts real knowledge as given by dreams. Even empirical investigation itself is coloured by one's paradigms: groups with different theories of how things work and different criteria for acceptable evidence could come to completely different conclusions from the same observation. Things even *look* different from within different paradigms.

One result of this way of thinking is the view that there's only a social explanation for whatever any group accepts as official truth; that is, there is no connection with the way things really are that explains this. A belief that's acceptable relative to our world-view, conceptual categories, and methodology, may be unacceptable relative to yours. There is no standpoint which allows us to judge *real* acceptability. In order for you to objectively criticize the views of some other group as false, you need some objective standards that apply to all belief-formation, by whatever group. But there are no such standards. All standards for judging beliefs as acceptable or not are part of the cognitive culture of a particular group, and may vary from group to group. So criticizing the cognitive procedures of a different group, using the standards of your own group, is just like complaining that a football player is violating the rules of baseball.

What this all implies is that there is no such thing as objective truth. It all depends on what group you belong to. This idea is called **relativism**.

Given the lack of any universal standards for belief-formation, the only way to get someone in a different cognitive society to agree with you is through force. Western society has a long history of doing this to other conquered cultures. This cognitive imperialism accompanies political and economic imperialism, and is often found very objectionable by modern enlightened people.

We see results of this sort of relativism and anti-imperialism in the way some people nowadays refer to the views of different cultures. For example:

> Western scientific archaeologists believe that the native American peoples emigrated from Asia, by boat or across a land-bridge to Alaska, tens of thousands of years ago. But the traditional stories of the North-American native peoples about their own origin are nothing like this. The origin story of the Navajo people of the American Southwest, for example, tells of their creation on the spot where they now live, where Turtle and Coyote created the earth and made six men and women out of it.

The relativistic/anti-imperialistic viewpoint we have been talking about refuses to characterize the anthropologists' story as knowledge, and the Navajos' story as mythology; each is true given its own criteria for truth – each deserves the approving title of 'knowledge'. So they urge that we speak of the 'traditional knowledge' of the native people, despite the fact that the propositions they are said to 'know' conflict from tribe to tribe, and with what Western scientists are said to 'know'. Whatever follows some society's standards for belief counts as 'knowledge'.

This position seems highly implausible to many people. After all, isn't there a fact of the matter about whether the North American native people originally came from Asia, or didn't? Relativists insist there isn't. They argue that what you take to be the fact of any matter depends on what your tests for real knowledge are. These vary from one group to another. There's no overriding, objectively correct methodology – no God's-eye-view. Nobody can stand outside every paradigm and see things 'as they really are' – the only way of seeing anything is from within one paradigm or another. That means that there isn't any such thing as the real fact of any matter.

Feminist epistemology

Feminist theory applied to epistemology has resulted in a wide variety of arguments and claims; but common to all of them is the idea that gender is an important (and historically neglected) consideration for the study, critique, and reconstruction of epistemology. Feminist epistemologists share the view that traditional epistemology is inadequate, assuming as it does that knowledge is to be seen in a pure, abstract, universal way, detached from the concrete realities of gender, social class, and other important differences.

Feminists often claim that the supposed universal abstract person considered by traditional epistemology is in fact male. There are practical instances of this, documented by feminists; for example, scientific projects which excluded women as the object of study or as researchers, ignoring perspectives and interests especially associated with women, or women's biology, or the things they're more likely to know. This sort of critique is often very telling, but it does not depend on any radical revision of the traditional demand for universality in epistemology and philosophy of science. These are examples of science which has flawed results because of *failure* of universality, in its own terms: bad science on the traditional view.

More theoretically radical, however, is the feminist criticism of the traditional value of objectivity. Traditional epistemology and philosophy of science presuppose that the best belief-formation processes are those that operate purely rationally, where rationality is supposed to exclude feelings and values. Letting one's emotions or values influence one's belief, after all, is traditionally supposed to make for biased or falsified or misinterpreted or inadequate data and interpretation, with bad consequences.

Many pre-feminist philosophers of science have admitted that the scientific researchers' values play important roles in research: in choice of questions to try to answer and in dreaming up hypotheses to test. Where strict objectivity is supposed to come into play is in the hypothesis-testing stage. But the feminist critique often insists on the place of values and attitudes in the testing of hypotheses too. Feminists (and other contemporary philosophers of science and epistemologists) sometimes claim that in every stage of science – in every stage of any cognitive activity of any sort that anybody does – there is inevitable influence by that person's values, attitudes, past experiences, emotional state, and so on. Mainstream epistemology has always advised against letting any of this interfere with truth-seeking. But some feminists think that it's inevitable that this sort of thing is involved in any epistemic activity, so the aim of objectivity is doomed. In fact, they claim, the official and institutionalized truth-seeking procedures have always been male dominated; so the values, attitudes, and so on that it has always reflected have been those typical of males.

Many feminists argue that the part played by these values and so on is not harmful, but that it's essential to epistemic activity and should be acknowledged and incorporated into a realist epistemology, and that the pretence of pure objectivity be dropped. Many argue that a true epistemic universality could be achieved only when characteristically female values, attitudes, experience, and so on, have been added to the determinants of epistemic activity and results.

Both feminist epistemology and the social relativism discussed above have been associated with the recent family of positions called **post-modernism**. This extremely varied (and often somewhat unintelligible) school is united by its rejection of the ideology of 'modernism' – the dominant ideology since Descartes – which emphasizes objectivity, universality, rationality, individualism, and truth. Post-modernists instead tend to concentrate on social and unconscious irrational determinants of the way we think and what we do.

A number of feminists are attracted to the idea of knowledge as *situated* – that what you count as knowledge depends on a large number of characteristics that vary from person to person, and especially from male to female. Suggested variables here include not just emotions, attitudes, interests, and values, but also:

Embodiment: different experiences depending on different body constitutions and locations;

Personal knowledge of others;

Know-how, especially practical know-how – in contrast to the propositional knowledge traditional epistemology has concentrated on;

Cognitive styles;

Background beliefs and world-views;

Knowledge-relations to other enquirers depending on whether one is an informant, interlocutor, student, teacher, supervisor, employee ...

It seems very clear now (though historically speaking, it has not been clear at all to many scientists and philosophers of science) that these sorts of things might be important in some scientific contexts – for example, that a sociological study of working women in industry should take care to involve researchers and data-collectors who are women (and people from working-class backgrounds as well). It would be far more controversial, however, to claim that the special situation of women makes it vital that they be included in research on, for example, mathematics or astronomy or subatomic physics. Some feminists agree that the gender situation of the knower has little if anything to do with knowledge in areas such as these.

Sometimes feminists argue that the ideals of rationality, objectivity, and truth are typically male, and a more balanced, more effective knowledge-seeking strategy would include procedures traditionally excluded, some of them sometimes considered 'female': gut-feelings, 'woman's intuition', know-how, what are called fallacies in informal reasoning, common-sense, anecdotal evidence (isolated personal experience), gossip, rumour ... You won't be surprised to hear that more traditional philosophers of science and epistemologists regard this as demonization of rationality – not merely bad strategic advice, but downright dangerous.

One problem in evaluating feminist proposals for epistemology is that a number of them are highly programmatic: changes are urged in incorporating feminist concerns, but details of what epistemology would look like when these changes have been made have sometimes not been worked out. The feminist project in epistemology is fairly young; there were historical precursors, but the main work in this area is only a couple of decades old. Some critics (including some feminists) believe it's still too early to have a good idea of what the result of a feminist revolution in epistemology would be supposed to bring.

In closing

In this last chapter, we have been looking at some far-reaching and basic critiques of epistemology as it has been carried on for centuries – even millennia. While there are a number of philosophers who find these radical positions exciting, they have by no means taken over the discipline. The traditional problems, and the modern attempts to deal with them using traditional philosophical techniques, are still the mainstream of epistemology. Theories examined in earlier chapters are still the ones philosophers are working on. In a number of cases, we've looked at some contemporary approaches to traditional problems that have been thought very promising; many epistemologists are now trying to elaborate and refine these.

In this book we've really (of course) only scratched the surface. Here we've dealt with questions and proposed answers in broad outline only. There is a great deal of philosophical literature available on every topic in this book. Now you know enough about the general philosophical lie-of-the-land, and about basic procedures and vocabulary, to read and understand this literature, to pursue issues that interest you. You will, no doubt, feel more attracted to some answers to our questions than to others, and that's how it should be; but you'll also have seen that each promising answer raises several more questions. What's hoped is that now you have a taste of what goes on in the fields, and that you'll be tempted to look further into the questions and answers that interest you. Following this chapter, there's advice on where to start looking. I hope you will.

Further reading

What should you read next?

Much philosophical writing is too technical or detailed to be the next step for those whose introduction to epistemology has been reading this book. Where you should go next is either to a **survey article** discussing the major positions and authors on that issue, or to a **classical position paper** – a widely known article that sets the terms for a debate, and produces the most persuasive arguments for one position.

Internet reference works

DO NOT TRUST WIKIPEDIA. What's there is a mixture of some useful information with a good deal of useless garble, inaccuracy, and blunder.

There are two good internet philosophy encyclopaedias that provide reliable short survey articles on many of the large and small topics we discuss. Each has a good index; but in the chapter-by-chapter listings below you'll see titles of some of the relevant articles in each.

SEP *The Stanford Encyclopedia of Philosophy*: http://plato.stanford. edu/. A source for reliable first-rate articles, but still incomplete. When you can find an article in here on what you're interested in, read it.

IEP *The Internet Encyclopedia of Philosophy*: http://www.iep.utm. edu/. Good but not as good as SEP, although more complete. Use as a supplement to the SEP, or as a fallback when an SEP article is not available.

The Routledge Encyclopedia of Philosophy is a good source, and is available on-line, but only by paid subscription, or perhaps through your university library; otherwise, in hard copy.

Paper reference works

CTE *A Companion to Epistemology* (Blackwell, 1992) Thorough, complete, reliable.

Useful big dictionaries and encyclopaedias on all philosophy are published by Blackwell, Cambridge University Press, and Oxford University Press.

Epistemology textbooks

These will have chapters corresponding to major topics in epistemology, usually at greater length, and in greater depth than in the book in your hands. It will be easy to find relevant sections in any of these. Some good ones available are:

ITE *Introduction to Epistemology*, by Jack Crumley (Broadview Press, 2009)

ECI *Epistemology: A Contemporary Introduction to the Theory of Knowledge*, by Robert Audi, Second Edition (Routledge, 2002)

ICE *An Introduction to Contemporary Epistemology*, by Jonathan Dancy (Blackwell, 1985)

Epistemic Justification, by Laurence BonJour and Ernest Sosa (Blackwell, 2003)

Epistemology: Classic Problems and Contemporary Responses, by Laurence BonJour (Rowman & Littlefield, 2002)

Epistemology, by Richard Feldman (Prentice-Hall, 2003)

Anthologies

These usefully juxtapose more than one article on each subject. Those listed contain excellent selections.

Classical and contemporary articles

TKCCR *The Theory of Knowledge, Classical and Contemporary Readings*, by Louis P. Pojman, ed., Third Edition (Wadsworth, 2003)

ECR *Epistemology: Contemporary Readings*, by Michael Huemer, ed. (Routledge, 2002)

Includes historical articles as well.

RTK *Readings in the Theory of Knowledge*, by John V. Canfield and Franklin H. Donnell, Jr, eds (Appleton-Century-Crofts, 1964)

Contemporary articles only

KRCE *Knowledge: Readings in Contemporary Epistemology*, by Sven Bernecker and Fred Dretske, eds (Oxford University Press, 2000)

EAA *Epistemology: An Anthology*, by Ernest Sosa et al., eds, Second Edition (Blackwell, 2008)

PP *Philosophical Perspectives 2: Epistemology*, by James Tomberlin, ed. (Ridgeview, 1988)

KNOW *Knowing: Essays in the Analysis of Knowledge*, by Michael D. Roth and Leon Gallis, eds (Random House, 1970)

The next two anthologies are unusual in that they contain articles specially written for them, by leading philosophers.

OHE *The Oxford Handbook of Epistemology*, by Paul K. Moser, ed. (Oxford University Press, 2002)

This may be available electronically through your university library.

BGE *The Blackwell Guide to Epistemology*, by John Greco and Ernest Sosa, eds (Blackwell, 1999)

Longer works by historical philosophers

EMP *Some Texts from Early Modern Philosophy*: http://www.earlymod-erntexts.com/

An exceptionally valuable on-line free source for longer works by historical philosophers; new very readable translations by Jonathan Bennett, with good explanations of obscurities inserted. Included at the moment are works by sixteen philosophers; of particular relevance to this book are works by Descartes, Hobbes, Locke, Berkeley, Hume, and Kant.

The Korcz List

Prof. Keith Korcz is the author of a useful on-line list of bibliographical references in epistemology. It's in the EPISTEMELINKS website at http://www.epistemelinks.com/Biblio/BiblioEpis.aspx. It includes a list of what he considers the ten most widely discussed papers in epistemology since 1963. Most are listed in the chapter-by-chapter section below, flagged by the notation *(KORCZ LIST)*.

Chapter-by-chapter sources and further reading

Here are listed the sources for quotations, together with suggestions for reading. In most cases articles listed can be found in one of the anthologies already mentioned.

Chapter 1

All these are good sources for surveys and arguments concerning issues in this chapter:

'An Introduction to the Analysis of Knowledge', by Jack Crumley, in
    ITE
'The Analysis of Knowledge', by Matthias Steup, in SEP
'Epistemology', by David A. Truncellito, in IEP (in Part 1 and first half
    of Part 2)
'What is Knowledge?', by Linda Zagzebski, in BGE
'Conditions and Analyses of Knowing', by Robert Shope, in OHE

Chapter 2

Ayer's ideas are found in *The Problem of Knowledge* (MacMillan, 1956);
the quotations are from Chapter 1, Sections iii and v. Selections from
this are in KNOW, ECR, and KRCE.

Descartes' *Meditations on First Philosophy* (1641) is his best-known
work, but *Rules for the Direction of the Mind* (1628?) is another important
source. Selections from *Meditations* are in TKCCR; from *Rules* in RTK.
The quotations in this chapter, however, are from his letters and replies,
collected in *Oeuvres de Descartes*, Charles Adam and Paul Tannery (eds)
(J. Vrin, 1904), Volume 3, pp. 64–5, and Volume 7, pp. 144–5.
Substantial portions of Descartes are in EMP. For summaries of
Descartes' epistemology see 'Descartes', Epistemology' by Lex Newman
in SEP, and 'Descartes, René' by John Cottingham, in CTE.

Several selections – none recent – on the issue of the necessity of
infallibility for knowledge are in Part One of RTK. See also 'How to
be a Fallibilist' by Stewart Cohen in PP. *(KORCZ LIST)*

These articles include good surveys of the issues in this chapter:

'What is Knowledge?', by Linda Zagzebski, in BGE
'Conditions and Analyses of Knowing', by Robert Shope, in OHE
'Epistemology', by David A. Truncellito, in IEP
'Epistemology', by Matthias Steup, in SEP

Chapter 3

Edmund L. Gettier's *(KORCZ LIST)* article 'Is Justified True Belief
Knowledge?', first published in 1963, is widely reprinted, including in

ECR, TKCCR, KRCE, and KNOW. ECR, KRCE, and TKCCR all contain good commentaries on Gettier, including 'Knowledge: Undefeated Justified True Belief' by Keith Lehrer and Thomas D. Paxson, Jr (The pyromaniac case is in here; *KORCZ LIST*.)

These articles survey the problem and its main responses:

'An Introduction to the Analysis of Knowledge', by Jack Crumley, in
　　ITE
'Gettier problem', by Paul K. Moser, in CTE
'Conditions and Analyses of Knowing', by Robert Shope, in OHE
'Knowledge', by Jonathan Dancy, in Chapter 2 of ICE
'Gettier Problems', by Stephen Hetherington, in IEP
'Epistemology', by David A. Truncellito, Part 2, in IEP
'Epistemology', by Matthias Steup, Part 1.2, in SEP

Chapter 4

Survey articles on the externalist/internalist distinction:

'Externalism/Internalism', by Laurence BonJour, in CTE
'Externalism and Internalism in Epistemology', by Ted Poston, in IEP
'Externalism and Internalism', by Jack Crumley, in ITE
'Internalism and Externalism', by Jonathan Dancy, Section 3.5, in ICE

Writers who favour internalism or externalism will produce arguments against the other one of the pair; so all the articles below (which favour internalism) will discuss both.

'Externalist Theories of Justification', by Laurence BonJour, in EAA
　　(KORCZ LIST)
'Epistemological Duties', by Richard Feldman, in OHE
'The Indispensability of Internal Justification', by Roderick M.
　　Chisholm, in KRCE
'A Critique of Externalism', by Keith Lehrer, in TKCCR

'The Deontological Conception of Epistemic Justification', by William P. Alston, in PP

The first Descartes quotation is from his *Regulae*, Rule III, ¶5. The second one is from his *Principles* I, 45.

The classical article on the causal theory is 'A Causal Theory of Knowing', by Alvin I. Goldman, in ECR, TKCCR, KNOW, and KRCE.

Survey articles on reliabilism:

'Reliabilism', by Alvin I. Goldman, in SEP
'Reliabilism', by Jack Crumley, in ITE

For a form of reliabilism, see 'Discrimination and Perceptual Knowledge', by Alvin I. Goldman, in KRCE. *(KORCZ LIST)*

The classical article on the truth-tracking theory is 'Knowledge', by Robert Nozick, in ECR.

The problem about red barns at the end of this chapter is known as the problem of epistemic closure. There are five articles on this problem in a section of EAA, including 'Epistemic Operators', by Fred Dretske. *(KORCZ LIST)*

Chapter 5

An article on both foundationalism and coherentism is 'The Architecture of Knowledge', by Robert Audi, in ECI.

Survey articles are:

'Foundationalism', by William P. Alston, in CTE
'Foundationalism' and 'Coherence Theories', both by Jonathan Dancy, in ICE
'Coherentism', by Keith Lehrer, in CTE
'Structure and Sources of Justification: Foundationalism' and 'Structure and Sources of Justification: Coherence Theory', both by Jack Crumley, in ITE

Robert Audi defends foundationalism in:

'The Sources of Knowledge', in OHE
'Contemporary Modest Foundationalism', in TKCCR

   Laurence BonJour defends coherentism and attacks foundationalism
in various articles in BGE, TKCCR, ECR, and KRCE. See especially
his 'Can Empirical Knowledge Have a Foundation?', in EAA.
(KORCZ LIST)
   The point about conspiracy theories is in ITE. Look at the website
of the Flat Earth Society, http://www.alaska.net/~clund/e_djublon-
skopf/Flatearthsociety.htm and see if you think they're joking.

Chapter 6

Survey articles about the a priori are:

'Reason', by Robert Audi, in ECI
'A Priori Knowledge', by Jonathan Dancy, in ICE
'A Priori/A Posteriori' and 'A Priori Knowledge', by Albert Casullo,
   in CTE
'*A Priori* Justification and Knowledge', by Bruce Russell, in SEP
'A Priori and A Posteriori', by Jason S. Baehr, in IEP

   For Plato's ideas about the forms and their epistemology see his
dialogues *Meno*, *Phaedo*, and *Theaetetus*, and his metaphorical stories of
the Sun, the Line, and the Cave in the *Republic*. Relevant excerpts from
Plato are in RTK and TKCCR. Articles about Plato's epistemology are:

'Plato', by Nicholas White, in CTE
'Plato on Knowledge in the *Theaetetus*', by Timothy Chappell, in SEP

   Kant's main work on the a priori is in his long and difficult *Critique
of Pure Reason*. Excerpts are in TKCCR and RTK. Kant also wrote on

this subject in *Prolegomena to Any Future Metaphysic*, excerpted in TKCCR and RTK. The best source for Kant for beginners is EMP.

Other articles on the a priori are:

'A Priori', by George Bealer, in BGE
'A Priori Knowledge', by Albert Casullo, in OHE

The Frege publication mentioned is *The Foundations of Arithmetic*, J. L. Austin, trans., Second Revised Edition, (Blackwell, 1959), §§5,88.

On non-Euclidian geometry in physics, see 'Appendix: Non-Euclidean Geometry and Relativity', by Laurence BonJour, in ECR.

The hugely influential Quine article (1951) is 'Two Dogmas of Empiricism', in TKCCR and ECR. The 'later writings' of Quine mentioned include *Word and Object* (MIT Press, 1964). The best-known reply to Quine's 'Two Dogmas' article is 'In Defense of a Dogma', by H. P. Grice and Peter F. Strawson, in TKCCR.

Kripke's argument about the metre bar is in *Naming and Necessity*, excerpted in KRCE.

The H_2O/XYZ example was proposed and discussed by Hilary Putnam in 'The meaning of "meaning"' in his *Philosophical Papers, Vol. 2: Mind, Language and Reality* (Cambridge University Press, 1975).

The theorist of possible-world thought mentioned is David Lewis. See his 'Counterfactual Dependence and Time's Arrow', *Nous*, 13, 1979, pp. 445–76.

Chapter 7

The Berkeley quotation is from *A Treatise Concerning the Principles of Human Knowledge*, Introduction, p. 10.

Quotations from Locke are all from his *Essay Concerning Human Understanding*; the one about introspection from 1:3, about the 'received doctrine' from 1:1; about the idea of God from 3:10; about cause from 3:17.

Hobbes's words are from *Leviathan*, 3:12.

The first quotation from Hume on God is from Section 2 of his *Enquiry of Human Understanding*. The second is from *The Letters of David Hume*, 2 Volumes, ed. by J. Y. T. Greig (Clarendon, 1932). I, 51 /#21.

For substantial portions of works by Hobbes, Locke, Berkeley, and Hume see EMP.

Surveys of the debate between rationalists and empiricists over the origin of concepts are in Section 4 of Peter Markie's 'Rationalism vs. Empiricism', and Section 3 of Eric Margolis's 'Concepts', both in SEP.

Perception is covered briefly in 'Perceptual Knowledge', by Fred Dretske, in CTE and extensively in articles by Audi in ECI, Crumley in ITE, Dancy in ICE, Crane in SEP, and O'Brien in IEP.

Chapter 8

The first Hume quotation on cause is from the *Enquiry*, Section 4, Part 1, and the second is from Section 4 Part 2, as is the quotation on past experience.

Survey articles on the problem of induction:

'Problems of Induction', by Laurence BonJour, in CTE
'Induction', by Jonathan Dancy, in ICE
'The Problem of Induction', by John Vickers, in SEP

Selections on the problem of induction from Hume and others are in ECR, TKCCR, RTK, and KRCE.

Discussions realist and anti-realist hypotheses are often embedded in a general discussion of scepticism. Survey articles that deal with these issues are:

'Scepticism', by Johathan Dancy, in ICE
'Problem of the External World', by George Pappas, 'Scepticism' and
    'Scepticism, Contemporary', both by Peter D. Klein, all in CTE
'Scepticism', by Jack Crumley, in ITE
    The 'Brain-in-the-Vat' example is in Hilary Putnam's *Reason, Truth*

and History (Cambridge University Press, 1982). It's excerpted in KRCE, and ECR.

Useful collections of articles on scepticism are in most epistemology anthologies, including KRCE, TKCCR, and EAA. See also 'Perceptual Knowledge', by William Alston and 'Scepticism', by Michael Williams, both in BGE.

Contextualism as a way of dealing with this scepticism is defended by Keith DeRose in 'Solving the Sceptical Problem', in *Philosophical Review* 104 (January 1995), pp. 1–52, but not in the anthologies listed here. *(KORCZ LIST)*

Chapter 9

Surveys on Naturalism and Naturalized Epistemology:

'Naturalism', by Philip Pettit and 'Naturalized Epistemology', by Hilary Kornblith, in CTE
'Naturalized Epistemology', by Richard Feldman, in SEP
'Naturalized Epistemology', by Jack Crumley, in ITE
'Naturalistic Epistemology', by Chase B. Wrenn, in IEP
'In Defense of a Naturalized Epistemology', by Hilary Kornblith and 'Methodological Naturalism in Epistemology', by Richard Feldman, in BGE

Quine's groundbreaking article is 'Epistemology Naturalized', in TKCCR and KRCE. See also Jaegwon Kim's 'What is "Naturalized Epistemology"?' in those two anthologies and in PP, and Alvin Goldman's 'The Sciences and Epistemology', in OHE.

The most interesting work by cognitive psychologists on how we in fact come to our beliefs is by Daniel Kahneman and Amos Tversky; their articles and others are in *Judgment Under Uncertainty: Heuristics and Biases*, edited by Kahneman et al. (Cambridge University Press, 1982).

'Evolutionary epistemology' is a survey by Edward Stein in CTE.

Kuhn's book is *The Structure of Scientific Revolutions* (University of Chicago Press, 1962).

Epistemology-as-sociology is surveyed by Alvin Goldman in 'Social Epistemology', in SEP, and by David Bloor in 'Sociology of Knowledge' and 'Strong Programme', in CTE. An article on this approach is 'Social Epistemology', by Frederick Schmitt, in BGE.

An overview of Postmodernism is Gary Aylesworth's 'Postmodernism', in SEP.

For surveys and other writings on feminist epistemology, see:

'Feminist Epistemology', by Helen E. Longino, in BGE
'Embodiment and Epistemology', by Louise Antony, in OHE
'Feminist Epistemology', by Jack Crumley, in ITE
'Feminist Epistemology and Philosophy of Science', by Elizabeth Anderson and 'Feminist Social Epistemology', by Heidi Grasswick, both in SEP. (The list of variables in 'situated' knowers is adapted from Anderson's article.)

Index